Betty Crocker's

Low-fat, Low-cholesterol

cooking today

An International Data Group Company

Foster City, CA • Chicago, IL • Indianapolis, IN • New York, NY

IDG BOOKS WORLDWIDE, INC.
An International Data Group Company
919 E. Hillsdale Boulevard
Suite 400
Foster City, CA 94404

For general information on IDG Books Worldwide's books in the U.S., please call our Consumer Customer Service department at 800-762-2974. For reseller information, including discounts and premium sales, please call our Reseller Customer Service department at 800-434-3422.

Cataloging-in-Publication Data available from the Library of Congress
ISBN: 0-02-863762-3

GENERAL MILLS, INC.
Betty Crocker Kitchens
Manager, Publishing: Lois L. Tlusty
Editor: Kelly Kilen
Recipe Development: Nancy Hughes
Food Stylists: Sue Finley, Mary H. Johnson, Katie McElroy
Nutritionist: Nancy Holmes, R.D.

Photographic Services
Photographer: Steven B. Olson

For consistent baking results, the Betty Crocker Kitchens recommend Gold Medal Flour.

Manufactured in the United States of America
10 9 8 7 6 5 4 3 2
Third Edition

Book Design: Scott Meola
Cover Design: Scott Meola and Michele Laseau
Art Director: Pam Kurtz
Cover: Glazed Beef Tenderloin with Herbed New Potatoes (page 96)

You've heard it once,
you've heard it twice.

You've heard it so many times you probably know it by heart—eating a diet low in fat, saturated fat and cholesterol can lower your risk of heart disease, and eating less fat helps you cut calories and shed some extra pounds. But did you know you can eat healthy and still enjoy the foods you love?

A healthy lifestyle isn't just about chopping all the fat and cholesterol from your diet. Healthy living means looking at the big picture. But for many of us, this means sorting through a lot of complicated, and sometimes contradictory, information about health and nutrition. With *Betty Crocker's Low-Fat, Low-Cholesterol Cooking Today*, we show you just how easy it can be to enter the world of healthy eating. All of the latest information on fat and cholesterol is brought to you in an easy-to-understand format, along with great tips and ideas to make eating a healthy diet a cinch to follow.

But on to the best part—the recipes. You'll find over 120 taste-tempting recipes that are packed full of flavor and geared for today's busy lifestyles. Plus we've marked every recipe with low fat, low cholesterol and low calorie designations, so you can find the recipes you want quickly. You'll also find helpful tips for cutting fat without skimping on taste. And to make meal planning a snap, we've added a week's worth of delicious menus guaranteed to win rave reviews from your family. Healthy eating has never been so delicious, or easy!

Betty Crocker

P.S. Here's to your health, with your heart in mind!

contents

Greek Salad Toss (page 147)

here's to your health

This book is all about eating well, which means eating foods that are good for you *and,* even more importantly, enjoying what you eat.

Just about everyone recognizes that healthy eating is a good idea, yet in a survey conducted by the American Dietetic Association, less than half of Americans felt that they were doing all they could to eat well. The three top reasons why were:

- A fear of having to give up favorite foods.

- It takes too much time.

- Information on health is contradictory.

Forget your fears! Healthy eating can be easy and convenient, and it can include your favorite foods. Though news reports and headlines may lead you to believe that certain foods are poor choices or that there are quick fixes to feeling great, in reality, common sense and balance are the mainstays of good health.

This book is about common sense and balance, and it's about putting the fun back into food. *Low-Fat, Low-Cholesterol Cooking Today* connects the dots between good taste, good food and good nutrition. You'll see, as you flip through the pages, that they connect perfectly.

DIET AND HEALTH—WHAT'S THE CONNECTION?

Thousands of studies have shown that diet has a significant impact on health, and new research continues to strengthen the link. Just how big an impact does diet has on health? Take a look:

- More than one-third of all cancers is attributed to diet.

- Three of the five major risk factors for heart disease (that are controllable), including blood cholesterol level, blood pressure and weight, are influenced by food.

- Many new research studies link certain vitamins, minerals and phytochemicals (naturally occurring substances in plant foods) with a lower risk for disease.

- Diet and inactivity result in 300,000 deaths in the United States each year.

- Seventy percent of the diagnosed cases of heart disease are related to obesity.

This is the short list. Diet and health are connected in many more ways. But enough of the startling statistics; it's time to look at what you can do to make your life healthier. At the top of the list is reducing fat and cholesterol in your diet. Fat and cholesterol are two of the most influential dietary components that affect your health. Both are associated with a higher risk for heart disease, and fat has been linked to other health problems, such as cancer and obesity. Too much fat and cholesterol are bad news, though that's not really *new* news. What is new, however, are all the things you can do to stay well and the creative ways you can reduce the amount of fat and cholesterol you eat.

So should you "worry" about fat and cholesterol? No. Instead, take the constructive approach to learn what you can do about fat and cholesterol to become well and stay that way. The payback, in terms of good health, is well worth the effort.

FAT FACTS

The story on fat is not all bad. Fat is a nutrient, just like protein, carbohydrate, vitamins and minerals. Fat helps keep us healthy because it:

- Provides linoleic acid, a fatty acid essential to proper growth, healthy skin and the metabolism or construction of cholesterol in the liver.

- Helps transport, absorb and store the fat-soluble vitamins A, D, E and K.

- Insulates and cushions body organs.

- Supplies energy. It's the most concentrated source of calories (9 calories per gram of fat versus 4 calories per gram for protein and carbohydrate).

- Satisfies us. Because fat takes longer to digest, it helps control hunger. It is responsible for the creamy texture of ice cream, the crispness of chips and French fries and the flavorful tastes of many other foods.

Sources of Fat

You don't have to search long or hard to find a few sources of fat in your food. Fat is found in meat, fish and poultry. It is also found in sauces, dressings, butter, margarine, oils, and even in plant sources like nuts and avocados. But don't let fat fool you; hidden fat is abundant too. Fat is an integral part of baked foods and many snack foods, and it can be found in all sorts of dairy foods.

Over the past forty years, Americans have cut back on the amount of fat they eat, and manufacturers have responded by developing thousands of low-fat or fat-free products. While many of these products have helped us cut our fat intake, we still have a ways to go on the fat front. Health experts recommend no

Sources of Fat in the Diet

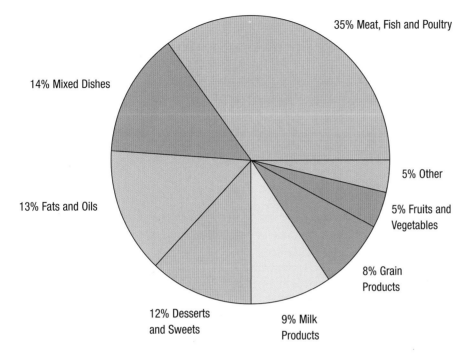

- 35% Meat, Fish and Poultry
- 14% Mixed Dishes
- 13% Fats and Oils
- 12% Desserts and Sweets
- 9% Milk Products
- 8% Grain Products
- 5% Fruits and Vegetables
- 5% Other

SOURCE: General Mills Dietary Intake Study, 1990–1992.

more than 30 percent of the calories you eat in a day come from fat.

The greatest amount of fat in the American diet comes from fats and oils, salad dressings, gravies, sauces and candy. The next source of fat in the diet is meat, fish and poultry. Look at the pie chart above, and you can see how fat fits into the daily diet.

TEST YOUR HEALTH IQ

True or false? Oil labeled "light" contains less fat and calories than regular oil.

ANSWER: False. All oils are 100 percent fat. One tablespoon of oil contains about 120 calories and nearly 14 grams of fat. When you see "light" on the label it refers to the color, not the fat or calorie content.

The Many Faces of Fat

All fats are made up of building blocks called fatty acids. Fatty acids are either saturated, monounsaturated or polyunsaturated.

Though some fats, such as monounsaturated and polyunsaturated may be "better" than others for your health, the best advice for eating well is to eat a diet low in all types of fat.

SATURATED VERSUS UNSATURATED FATS

Saturated fats are solid at room temperature and are found primarily in foods from animal sources. Foods that contain higher amounts of saturated fats include meats, eggs and dairy products (whole milk, hard cheese, butter and cream). Tropical fats (coconut, palm and palm kernel oils) are considered

THE SKINNY ON HDLS AND LDLS

Cholesterol is shuttled around the body by substances called low-density lipoproteins (LDLs). LDLs carry cholesterol from the liver (where it is formed) to cells throughout the body. LDLs can deposit excess amounts of cholesterol on the walls of various arteries in your body. These deposits are a form of plaque, which over time can build up, narrow the openings inside arteries and lead to heart disease. This action has earned LDLs the title "bad cholesterol."

Another carrier of cholesterol in the blood is called high-density lipoproteins (HDLs). HDLs are scavengers. They can carry excess cholesterol away from the artery walls and back to the liver for reprocessing or removal from the body. HDLs help to prevent cholesterol buildup and are therefore referred to as "good" cholesterol.

saturated fatty acids, yet they are unique because they come from plants. Health experts recommend saturated fat is limited to 10 percent of calories or less each day.

The downside of saturated fats. Research demonstrates a solid link between a diet high in saturated fats and the incidence of high blood cholesterol. Saturated fats raise low-density lipoprotein (LDL) cholesterol in the blood (the artery-clogging cholesterol). Eating saturated fats raises blood cholesterol more than eating any other type of fat, and more than the actual cholesterol found in food.

Unsaturated fats come primarily from plant sources. They are usually liquid at room temperature. There are two types of unsaturated fats, monounsaturated and polyunsaturated. Olive oil, canola oil and peanut oil are high in monounsaturated fats; corn, soybean, safflower and sunflower oils contain proportionately more polyunsaturated fats.

All foods that contain fat are actually made up of mixtures of saturated and unsaturated (monounsaturated and/or polyunsaturated) fatty acids. In fact, even fats such as cooking oils and margarine contain a mixture of the three.

The upside of unsaturated fats. When unsaturated fats replace saturated fats in the diet, blood cholesterol levels can go down. Polyunsaturated fats can also help lower blood cholesterol levels by lowering LDL cholesterol. Unfortunately, they also lower HDL cholesterol (the good cholesterol that can remove plaque from artery walls). Monounsaturated fats, on the other hand, help more. They lower LDL cholesterol and may actually increase HDL cholesterol. The key to success for either of these fats is a diet low in total fat, and particularly low in saturated fat.

WAIT, THERE'S MORE. . .

Two other types of fat that affect your health are *trans fatty acids* and *omega-3 fats.*

Trans fatty acids (TFA) are formed during hydrogenation—a process that changes liquid fats into a more solid and saturated form. Food manufacturers use hydrogenated fats because they improve the shelf life and stability of a product. Highly unsaturated vegetable oils, such as safflower or sunflower oil, are not stable enough to use in some food products because they develop "off flavors" within a short period of time. Check the labels of cookies, snack foods and bakery products. You'll see that many list "hydrogenated" oil as one of the ingredients.

The downside of trans fats. When it comes to blood cholesterol levels, trans fats act more like a saturated fat than the unsaturated fat they started out as. Trans fats are believed to raise blood cholesterol levels, including LDL cholesterol, and lower

HDL cholesterol levels when they are substituted for polyunsaturated fats in the diet. But when trans fats are substituted for saturated fats, research has found that cholesterol levels can fall. Some research has also linked trans fats with an increased risk for certain cancers.

Omega-3 fats, often referred to as *fish oils*, are unsaturated fats found primarily in certain kinds of fish, particularly salmon, mackerel, trout and albacore tuna. They are also found in high concentrations in flax seed, which is not especially common but is finding its way on to the shelves of many health food stores. The seeds have a high oil content and are sometimes ground into a flour, mixed with liquid and used to add body to baked goods.

The upside of omega-3 fats. Studies show omega-3 fatty acids may reduce the risk for heart disease and stroke by lowering blood cholesterol levels and decreasing the likelihood of clots forming in the blood. How much of an impact do they have? One study found that middle-aged men who ate the equivalent of an ounce of fish a day were 44 percent less likely to have a heart attack than men who did not eat fish. The American Heart Association (AHA) recommends eating several servings of fish a week. If fish is not a favorite in your family, other good sources for omega-3 fats are soybean and canola oils.

WHAT'S THE BOTTOM LINE?

Too much of any kind of fat, including the fats classified as "good," such as olive oil and fish oils, can sabotage your efforts to eat well. If you reduce all fats in your diet and eat proportionately more unsaturated fat than saturated, you'll be on the right track for good health. (See Fat Trimming Tips on page 13).

COMPARING FATS AND OILS

Fat Source	Saturated (%)	Monounsaturated (%)	Polyunsaturated (%)	Cholesterol (mg/Tablespoon)
Canola Oil	6	62	32	0
Safflower Oil	9	12	75	0
Sunflower Oil	10	20	66	0
Corn Oil	13	24	59	0
Olive Oil	14	74	8	0
Margarine, stick	14	39	24	0
Margarine, soft tub	14	32	31	0
Soybean Oil	15	43	38	0
Peanut Oil	17	46	32	0
Vegetable Shortening	25	45	26	0
Palm Oil	49	37	9	0
Butter	62	29	4	33
Coconut Oil	87	6	2	0

Source: Duyf, Roberta L. *The American Dietetic Association's Complete Food and Nutrition Guide.* Minneapolis: Chronimed Publishing, 1998.

REDUCING FAT IN THE DIET

Currently, about 34 percent of the calories in the average American diet come from fat. This represents about 75 grams of total fat in a typical 2,000-calorie diet. That is the equivalent of 5 tablespoons (or more than 1/4 cup) of solid margarine per day.

The AHA and many other health organizations recommend that healthy adults reduce their total fat intake to less than 30 percent of calories a day (about 65 grams in a 2,000-calorie diet). Keep in mind this guideline applies to an entire day's worth of foods, not to a single food or recipe. For example, you might eat a low-fat breakfast and lunch and then splurge on a small piece of chocolate cake for dessert. Even though the cake may not be a low-fat food, that's okay as long as it fits into your total fat or calorie budget for the day. You don't have to go totally fat free, nor is it advised that you cut out all fats from your diet. To maintain a healthy diet, it is most important to look at what you eat over the long haul.

UNDERSTANDING CHOLESTEROL

What is cholesterol? Cholesterol is a soft, waxy, fat-like substance produced by the liver. The body makes 800 to 1,500 milligrams of cholesterol each day, which circulates through the bloodstream.

Cholesterol has many functions:

- It is an essential part of every cell in your body.

- It helps to produce certain hormones, such as estrogen.

KIDS AND FAT

When it comes to a low-fat eating plan young children are the exception to the rule. Children younger than age two should not have the amounts of fat and cholesterol in their diets restricted. Both fat and cholesterol are needed for growth and development, including brain development. Because of the small size of their stomachs, babies and kids younger than two are limited in the amount of food they can eat, and fat helps ensure they satisfy their calorie needs.

As a child grows and develops between the ages of two and five, it's okay to gradually decrease the fat in their diet. Replace some of the calories from fat with lower fat, nutrient-dense foods such as grains, fruits, vegetables, low-fat dairy products and other protein-rich sources.

By the time a child reaches age five, his or her eating style should follow the same Dietary Guidelines as older children and adults, limiting fat to no more that 30 percent of total calories and saturated fat to no more than 10 percent of total calories.

Higher-fat foods can still be part of a child's healthy diet. They add flavor and variety to a balanced diet and fuel the growth of active kids. The key is moderation and to watch the total fat in food choices over a period of several days, weeks and months.

FAT TRIMMING TIPS

Eat fewer high-fat foods. Eating less *visible* fat, such as salad dressings, margarine and sour cream, helps. Keep added fats and oils to 5 to 8 teaspoons per day. Try reduced-fat products for these foods.

Trim visible fat from meat, and remove the skin from chicken and turkey before eating. Cutting back on foods high in *hidden* fat, such as chips, high-fat cheeses and many bakery goods is important too.

Eat smaller portions. As portions grow, so too does their fat content. Skip the super-size meals and snacks, and choose normal-size servings.

Cook lean. Broil, bake, roast, grill, poach, steam, stew or even microwave foods whenever possible. You can stir-fry, too, if you use small amounts of unsaturated oils, such as canola or safflower oil. Use nonstick cookware and cooking spray to lessen the amounts of fat needed in cooking. Broths and vegetable juices are good sauté substitutes for oil, shortening and margarine.

Choose meatless meals at least twice each week. Limiting the amount of meat, fish and poultry you eat can help reduce fat, particularly saturated fat, while increasing fiber and complex carbohydrates. Trade meats for dried beans and peas, grains, vegetables and fruits. Go easy on the margarine, mayonnaise and cream sauces.

Select chicken, turkey or fish. Light-meat chicken and turkey are naturally low in fat, especially if you remove the skin. Most fish is also very lean. Even higher-fat fish, such as salmon, is as lean or leaner than poultry and lean beef. Some fish also have the added benefit of omega-3 fatty acids.

Use low-fat or fat-free dairy products. Many milk products contain a great deal of fat, especially if they are made with whole milk or cream. Choose from the many low-fat and fat-free dairy products available, such as low-fat yogurts, cheese, puddings, milk and ice cream.

- It is a vital part of your nervous system and brain.

- Through sunlight, it is converted to vitamin D in your skin.

- It helps in the digestion and absorption of fat.

While your body makes its own cholesterol, there is also cholesterol in the food we eat. Dietary cholesterol (the cholesterol in food) is found *only* in animal foods, such as cheese, meat, butter and eggs. Plant foods—grains, fruits, vegetables, nuts—do *not* contain cholesterol. Unlike fat, cholesterol does not contain any calories, nor is it a source of energy.

About one-third of Americans is sensitive to dietary cholesterol, meaning that eating foods high in cholesterol raises cholesterol levels in the blood. Currently there is no test to determine if you are the "sensitive type," therefore, health experts recommend everyone choose a diet that contains no more than 300 milligrams of cholesterol each day.

The easiest way to control dietary cholesterol is to learn which foods are high sources. The most concentrated sources of *dietary* cholesterol are organ meats, such as liver, brain and kidney, egg yolks and some high-fat dairy products, such as sour cream. (The table beginning on page 225 lists the cholesterol content of some familiar foods.) Compare the different foods so you will be able to choose wisely.

What's Your Cholesterol Number?

Measuring blood to determine the amount of cholesterol in it helps screen people for their risk for heart disease. For some people, however, just knowing total blood cholesterol may not be enough; finding out about LDL and HDL levels is also necessary.

SMART FOOD CHOICES

Food Category	Choose More	Choose Less
Breads, Cereals	Whole-grain, whole wheat, pumpernickel and rye breads; breadsticks; English muffins; bagels; rice cakes; pita breads	Croissants, butter rolls
	Oat bran, oatmeal, whole-grain cereals	Presweetened cereals
	Saltines, pretzels, zwieback, plain popcorn	Cheese crackers, butter crackers
Rice, Pasta	Rice, pasta	Egg noodles
Baked Goods	Angel food cake	Frosted cakes, sweet rolls, pastries, doughnuts
Fruits	Fresh, frozen or dried fruits	Fruit pies
Vegetables	Fresh or frozen vegetables	Vegetables prepared with butter, cream or cheese sauces
Meat, Poultry	Lean meats, skinless poultry	Fatty meats, organ meats, cold cuts, sausages, hot dogs
Fish	Fish, shellfish	
Beans, Peas	Split peas, kidney beans, navy beans, lentils, soybeans, tofu	
Eggs	Egg whites, fat-free cholesterol-free egg product	Egg yolks
Milk, Cream	Fat-free (skim) milk, 1% milk, low-fat or fat-free buttermilk	Whole milk, 2% milk, half-and-half, whipped toppings, most nondairy creamers, sour cream
Cheese	Fat-free or low-fat cottage cheeses, farmer cheese	Whole-milk cottage cheese, hard cheese, fat-free or low-fat cheeses, cream cheese
Yogurt	Fat-free or low-fat yogurt	Whole-milk yogurt
Frozen Desserts	Fat-free or low-fat ice cream, sherbet, fat-free or low-fat frozen yogurt	Ice cream
Fats, Oils	Polyunsaturated or monounsaturated vegetable oils: sunflower, corn, soybean, olive, safflower, sesame, canola, cottonseed	Saturated fats: coconut oil, palm oil, palm kernel oil, lard, bacon fat
Spreads	Margarine or shortening made with polyunsaturated fat	Butter
Chocolate	Cocoa	Chocolate

Source: Adapted from *The American Heart Association Diet: An Eating Plan for Healthy Americans,* American Heart Association.

(See The Skinny on HDLs and LDLs on page 10.) This is especially true for people whose total blood cholesterol is considered borderline-high (above 200 milligrams per deciliter of blood) and high (above 240 milligrams).

Physicians often will obtain LDL and HDL readings for nearly all their patients. A blood profile can determine the levels of LDLs and HDLs. This type of analysis may be advisable for people with borderline-high cholesterol levels plus two risk factors for heart disease (see table below).

Some physicians may calculate a ratio between HDL and total cholesterol. This is another approach to determining heart disease risk. However, the American Heart Association recommends focusing on absolute numbers for total blood cholesterol and HDL cholesterol levels.

A direct relationship exists between total blood cholesterol and LDL cholesterol, meaning as total blood cholesterol increases, so does LDL cholesterol. Three known causes of a high LDL and blood cholesterol level are:

- Genetic factors and family history

- A diet high in saturated fats and cholesterol

- Health conditions, such as diabetes, diseases of the liver and kidney or an underactive thyroid.

RISK FACTORS FOR CORONARY HEART DISEASE (CHD)

High blood cholesterol	Cigarette smoking
High blood pressure	Vascular disease
Family history of coronary heart disease before the age of 55	Obesity
	Being male
Sedentary lifestyle	Diabetes

WHAT DO THE NUMBERS MEAN?

Cholesterol (mg/dl)	Classification
Total less than 200	Desirable
Total 200 to 239	Borderline–High Risk
Total above 239	High Risk
LDL less than 130	Desirable
LDL 130 to 159	Borderline–High Risk
LDL above 159	High Risk
HDL above 35	Desirable

Source: National Heart, Lung and Blood Institute's National Cholesterol Education Program (NCEP).

Ounce for ounce, which has more cholesterol, prime rib or a chicken breast?

ANSWER: They are nearly the same. Both contain approximately 85 milligrams of cholesterol. Where they differ substantially is in their fat content. A 3-ounce portion of prime rib contains over 30 grams of fat, and a 3-ounce portion of chicken breast with skin contains 8 grams of fat. Take the skin off, and the fat content dips to 3 grams and cholesterol drops to 75 milligrams.

Just as heart disease risk increases with a high LDL and total blood cholesterol level, a low level of HDLs may indicate an increased risk for heart disease even if your total cholesterol is below 200 mg/dl. Some possible causes include lack of exercise, obesity, smoking and high blood cholesterol and/or triglycerides (another type of fat in the blood).

More than 50 percent of all adult Americans have blood cholesterol levels higher than 200 mg/dl, the "desirable" level; half of these people have levels above 240 mg/dl. Their risk for heart disease is double that of people whose cholesterol is below 200 mg/dl.

OTHER IMPORTANT NUTRIENTS

Besides fat and cholesterol, many other diet-related factors affect your health. Unlike fat and cholesterol, where the emphasis is on cutting back or limiting foods, most of the nonfat advice for a healthy eating plan involves adding foods to your menu and increasing their contributions to your diet. Some of the key heart-helping players include fiber, vitamin E and folic acid.

Fiber

Fiber is roughage. It's the skins, seeds and hulls found in plant foods, such as fruits, vegetables and grains. Fiber can be divided into two types, *soluble* and *insoluble* fiber.

Soluble fiber, as its name implies, dissolves in water. Soluble fiber slows the rate of digestion (how quickly the stomach empties), and it lowers the amount of insulin needed to take care of the food you have

CHOLESTEROL TRIMMING TIPS

Opt for a meatless meal at least twice each week. Since all meats and meat products contain cholesterol, a meatless meal is an easy way to keep your dietary cholesterol in check.

Be seafood savvy. Shellfish vary in their cholesterol content. Shrimp for example are very high in cholesterol, while scallops and mussels are quite low. All shellfish are low in total fat and saturated fat, which means that you can still eat them as part of a low-fat, low-cholesterol diet. Just make sure that you stay within your daily cholesterol limits.

Limit organ meats such as liver, brain and kidney. These meats are extremely high in cholesterol and should be eaten sparingly. Instead choose lean cuts of meats.

Limit eggs to four per week. The 210 milligrams of cholesterol in one egg yolk supplies more than two-thirds the recommended daily limit. The good news is that egg *whites* have no cholesterol, and in many cases can be used instead of whole eggs. For example, try an omelet made with one whole egg and two egg whites or use 1/4 cup fat-free cholesterol-free egg product.

Choose fat-free or low-fat dairy products. Dairy products can be cholesterol culprits. Choose a cup of fat-free (skim) milk instead of whole milk and save 30 milligrams of cholesterol. Replace a 1/2 cup of sour cream with a 1/2 cup of low-fat yogurt and cut your dietary cholesterol by 70 milligrams.

FIBER-FULL FOODS

Foods containing 6 or more grams of fiber:	Foods containing 4 to 5 grams of fiber:	Foods containing 2 to 3 grams of fiber:
1 cup cooked kidney, black or baked beans	1 pear	1 ounce peanuts
1 cup bran cereal	1 large apple	1/3 cup raisins
5 dried figs	1 medium baked potato with skin	1/2 cup cooked brown rice
1 cup raspberries	3 dried prunes	1 medium sweet potato
2 ounces uncooked whole wheat spaghetti	1 medium avocado	1/2 cup corn
	1 orange	2/3 cup flake or oat cereal

eaten. Soluble fiber may also lower total blood cholesterol, when it is part of a low-fat diet. It is believed to bind with cholesterol-carrying substances in the blood and escort them out of the body.

Insoluble fiber helps keep food moving through your digestive system. The more fiber you eat, the better shape your digestive system is in and the more smoothly foods move through your body. Several studies have shown that fiber may also lower the risk for some cancers, including colon cancer.

Both soluble and insoluble fiber may help you keep your weight in line, too. Fiber is filling, and because it slows digestion, you feel full longer. Foods high in fiber also tend to be naturally low in fat, such as fruits, veggies and whole grains.

Currently, there is no official Recommended Dietary Allowance (RDA) for fiber, but the Daily Value (DV) set by the Food and Drug Administration (FDA) is 25 grams a day. Most Americans get half of that amount.

How do you get to 25 grams of fiber? It's easy if you fill your day with five or more servings of fruits and vegetables or six or more servings of whole-grain breads, cereals and legumes (peas, beans, and lentils).

Vitamin E

Vitamin E shows a lot of promise as an important health-promoting nutrient. It is an antioxidant, which means it may be helpful in protecting the body from the damage caused by free radicals. Free radicals are believed to damage cells and DNA (your

TEST YOUR HEALTH IQ

Which of the following is the best source of antioxidants?

   a. Nuts

   b. Green tea

   c. Orange juice

   d. Sweet potatoes

ANSWER: b. Whether you prefer it ice cold or steaming hot, green tea is an antioxidant powerhouse. New research shows that green tea contains a powerful antioxidant, one some scientists believe is 100 times more potent than vitamin C and 25 times more effective than vitamin E.

Antioxidants may help reduce the risk for heart disease and some cancers by protecting the cells in your body from damage.

body's code for reproducing cells). The damage these free radicals cause may lead to health problems, such as heart disease, cancer, cataracts and more.

Few foods are good sources of vitamin E, and those that are, tend to be high in fat, such as vegetable oils, margarine and nuts. Whole-grain foods contain a small amount of vitamin E. The amount of vitamin E recommended for health promotion ranges from 100 International Units (IU) to 400 IU or more. Because food levels are significantly less, many people turn to supplements to cash in on vitamin E's possible benefits. Before you do, check with your doctor. Fatigue and flu-like symptoms have been seen with levels above 800 IU.

Vitamin E is not the only antioxidant vitamin. Vitamin C and beta carotene (a form of vitamin A) have also been shown to have potential health-promoting properties. However, the data on the role of these vitamins is fairly limited.

Folic Acid

Research shows that folic acid along with vitamin B_6 may work together to help heart health by lowering homocysteine levels in the blood. Homocysteine is an amino acid that moves through the blood much as cholesterol does. Normally, folic acid, vitamin B_6 and other B vitamins help break down homocysteine. However, a genetic defect or a diet low in these nutrients can result in a buildup of homocysteine, which in turn may injure arteries in the body and lead to their clogging.

Eating a diet rich in folic acid and B_6 may help keep homocysteine from becoming an issue. Foods rich in these two nutrients include whole grains, fortified cereals and legumes.

PUTTING IT ALL TOGETHER

The body needs more than forty different nutrients for good health. How do you keep track of them all?

Fortunately, someone has come up with a plan for figuring out what to eat. It's called the Food Guide Pyramid.

The Food Guide Pyramid

Think of the Food Guide Pyramid as the road map for eating well. It emphasizes variety in your food choices from the five major food groups and shows you in what proportions to eat them.

The *Bread, Cereal, Rice and Pasta Group* provides carbohydrate, iron and B vitamins (thiamin, riboflavin and niacin). Servings from this group include one ounce (about 3/4 cup) of breakfast cereal, one slice of bread, 1/2 cup cooked pasta or rice and 1/2 cup cooked cereal. Everyone needs *six to eleven servings* of these foods daily.

The *Vegetable Group* is made up of—surprise—vegetables. This group provides fiber, carbohydrate, folic acid, beta-carotene and vitamin C. One cup raw leafy vegetables, 1/2 cup cooked vegetables and 3/4 cup tomato juice are some examples of servings. Eat *three to five servings* from this group each day.

The *Fruit Group* supplies primarily fiber, carbohydrate, beta-carotene and vitamin C from fruit and juices. Everyone needs *two to four servings* of these foods each day. One medium piece of fruit, 1/2 cup of grapes or berries, 1/4 cup dried fruit (such as raisins) or 3/4 cup fruit juice are typical servings.

Iron, protein, niacin, zinc, vitamin B_6 and vitamin B_{12} (from animal sources only) come from the *Meat, Poultry, Fish, Dry Beans, Eggs and Nuts Group. Two to three servings* daily are enough for adults. One serving is 2 or 3 ounces of cooked lean protein (beef, poultry and fish), one egg and 2 tablespoons of peanut butter or 1/2 cup of cooked legumes (beans or peas).

We should eat *two to three servings* from the *Milk, Yogurt and Cheese Group* each day. This group offers calcium, phosphorus, protein and vitamins A

Food Guide Pyramid

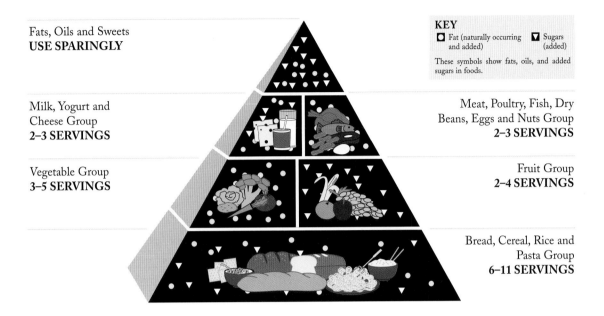

Fats, Oils and Sweets
USE SPARINGLY

KEY
☐ Fat (naturally occurring and added)   ▼ Sugars (added)

These symbols show fats, oils, and added sugars in foods.

Milk, Yogurt and
Cheese Group
2–3 SERVINGS

Meat, Poultry, Fish, Dry
Beans, Eggs and Nuts Group
2–3 SERVINGS

Vegetable Group
3–5 SERVINGS

Fruit Group
2–4 SERVINGS

Bread, Cereal, Rice and
Pasta Group
6–11 SERVINGS

Source: U.S. Department of Agriculture, U.S. Department of Health and Human Services.

and D. One serving includes 1 cup of milk, 1 cup of yogurt or 1 1/2 ounces of cheese. Young adults (to age 24), pregnant women and those who are breast-feeding need three servings daily.

The *Fats, Oils and Sweets Group* provides fatty acids and vitamin E. But avoid too much from this group, especially if you're trying to lose weight or keep your heart healthy.

By eating the recommended number of servings daily from the Food Guide Pyramid, you can ensure you will meet your needs for the many essential nutrients. Keep in mind, however, when the food groups were first devised, nutrient *deficiencies* were a concern. Today, we're more likely to be getting too much of certain nutrients rather than too little.

The Dietary Guidelines

If you consider the Food Guide Pyramid as the "picture" of a healthy diet, then the Dietary Guidelines, developed by the Department of Health and Human Services and the United States Department of Agriculture, tell the story. There are seven Dietary Guidelines for healthy eating.

Guideline #1   Eat a variety of foods.

No one food contains all the nutrients you need for good health. The more different kinds of foods you eat, the better for your body.

Guideline #2   Maintain a healthy weight.

Keeping your weight in line reduces your chances for several diseases, including heart disease, diabetes and stroke. Eating according to the Food Guide Pyramid is a terrific start to helping control calories.

Guideline #3   Choose a diet low in fat, saturated fat and cholesterol.

If you do, you reduce your risk for all sorts of diseases. Limiting fat is the quickest way to keep calories in line and weight where you want it to be.

Guideline #4 *Choose a diet with plenty of vegetables, fruits and grain products.*

These foods provide the vitamins, minerals and fiber essential for good health, plus they contain certain substances, such as phytochemicals, which may significantly lower your risk for cancer and other illnesses.

Guideline #5 *Use sugars only in moderation.*

In and of itself, sugar really does not cause health problems; but in excess, sugar can contribute unnecessary calories. Too much sugar can also lead to tooth decay.

Guideline #6 *Use salt and sodium only in moderation.*

Eating too much sodium may increase your risk for high blood pressure. Some studies suggest that too much sodium may also be bad for your bones because it may increase the amount of calcium lost from your body.

Guideline #7 *If you drink alcoholic beverages, do so in moderation.*

Alcohol contains calories but not much else. Some studies have indicated it may be good for your heart. Recommendations are for moderation (not more than one or two drinks per day).

As you make your food choices, consider how much fat and cholesterol they have. Also, think about their fiber, vitamin and mineral contents. Every choice does not have to be a perfect choice; some of your favorite foods may be big on taste and low on nutrition. Overall, make the foods you choose ones that will contribute positively toward your health.

FIND OUT ABOUT YOUR FOOD

As life continues to quicken in pace and fewer people take time to prepare foods from scratch, reading and understanding the information manufacturers provide about the nutritional content of their products becomes increasingly important. Once you learn how to read labels, you can make smart food choices.

Reading a Nutrition Label

The Nutrition Facts label is found on food packages in your supermarket. Reading the label tells you more about the food and the nutrients it supplies. The government requires the nutrition and ingredient information you see on the food label.

Some food packages have a short or abbreviated nutrition label. These foods contain only a few of the nutrients required on the standard label and can use a short label format. What's on the label depends on what's in the food. Small- and medium-size packages with very little label space also may use a short label format.

Nutrition Facts Label

Here's what the label looks like with an explanation of its new features.

NUTRITION FACTS TITLE
The new title "Nutrition Facts" signals the new label.

SERVING SIZE
Serving sizes are standardized based on amounts people actually eat. Now similar food products have similar serving sizes making it easier to compare foods in the same category.

NEW LABEL INFORMATION
Some label information may not be familiar to you. The nutrient list covers those nutrients most important to your health. You may have seen this information on some old labels, but now it is required by the government and must appear on all food labels.

VITAMINS AND MINERALS
The Percent Daily Value replaces the Percent U.S. RDA for vitamins and minerals. The levels are the same. Only vitamin A, vitamin C, calcium, iron, and fortified nutrients are required on the new label. Additional vitamins and minerals can be listed voluntarily.

LABEL NUMBERS
Numbers on the nutrition label may be rounded for labeling.

Nutrition Facts

Serving Size 1 cup (30g)
Servings Per Container About 10

Amount Per Serving

Calories 110   Calories from Fat 10

% Daily Value*

Total Fat 1g	**2%**
Saturated Fat 0g	**0%**
Cholesterol 0mg	**0%**
Sodium 240mg	**10%**
Total Carbohydrate 24g	**8%**
Dietary Fiber 3g	**10%**
Sugars 6g	
Protein 3g	

Vitamin A 25%	*	Vitamin C 25%
Calcium 4%	*	Iron 45%

* Percent Daily Values are based on a 2,000 calorie diet. Your daily values may be higher or lower depending on your calorie needs:

		Calories:	2,000	2,500
Total Fat	Less than		65g	80g
Sat. Fat	Less than		20g	25g
Cholesterol	Less than		300mg	300mg
Sodium	Less than		2,400mg	2,400mg
Total Carbohydrates			300g	375g
Dietary Fiber			25g	30g

Calories per gram:
Fat 0   *   Carbohydrate 4   *   Protein 4

% DAILY VALUE
The Percent Daily Value shows how a food fits into a 2,000 calorie reference diet. These levels are based on dietary recommendations for most healthy people. Percent Daily Values help you judge whether a food contains "a lot" or "a little" of key nutrients important to health.

DAILY VALUES FOOTNOTE
Daily Values are the new label reference numbers. These numbers are set by the government and are based on current nutrition recommendations. Some labels list Daily Values for a diet of 2,000 and 2,500 calories per day. Your own nutrient needs may be less than or more than the Daily Values on the label.

CALORIES PER GRAM FOOTNOTE
Some labels tell the appropriate number of calories in a gram of fat, carbohydrate, and protien. (One gram is about the weight of a regular paperclip.) This information helps you calculate the percentage of calories from these nutrients.

LABEL NUTRITION CLAIMS

Now, you can believe the claims on the food labels. Some food packages make claims such as "light," "low fat," and "cholesterol free." Keep in mind that these claims are for packaged food products, not necessarily recipes, and can be used only if a food meets strict government definitions. Here are some of the meanings:

Label Claim	Definition (per serving)
Low Calorie	40 calories or fewer
Light (or Lite)	1/3 fewer calories *or* 50 percent less fat than the original product; if more than half the calories are from fat, fat content must be reduced by 50 percent or more
Light in Sodium	50 percent less sodium
Fat Free	Less than 0.5 gram of fat
Low Fat	3 grams or fewer of fat
Cholesterol Free	Fewer than 2 milligrams of cholesterol and 2 grams or fewer of saturated fat
Low Cholesterol	20 milligrams or fewer of cholesterol and 2 grams or fewer of saturated fat
Sodium Free	Fewer than 5 milligrams of sodium
Very Low Sodium	35 milligrams or fewer of sodium
Low Sodium	140 milligrams or fewer of sodium
High Fiber	5 grams or more of fiber

GO SLOW FOR SUCCESS

When changing habits, whether it's eating, activity or other health-promoting plans, realizing the value of making gradual changes is important. You've spent a lifetime developing your current habits; if you expect to change all of them overnight, you may be disappointed.

Success is greatest for those who set realistic goals, thoughtfully plan their strategies for reaching their goals, and then break their goals into small, doable steps. Take on one or two challenges, and give yourself time to adjust to the changes. Small changes can turn into new lifetime habits that herald good health.

Plan strategies that will help you overcome your hurdles. For example, if you eat too many high-fat foods and too few fruits, vegetables and complex carbohydrates, resolve to eat apple wedges, red bell pepper rings or pretzels instead of chips with your noontime sandwich. Change your standard breakfast to fat-free (skim) milk, cereal and fruit instead of doughnuts or pastries. Cut back on the amount of meat you eat by preparing meals that are combinations of vegetables, meat and complex carbohydrates such as mixed rice or pasta dishes. Remember, there's no need to completely forgo your favorite foods. You can continue to eat these foods occasionally.

Once you have control over the problem areas at the top of your list, move on to other areas that you think needs improvement. If even after reducing the amount of fat in your diet, you find that you're still eating a bit too much and consequently weigh more than you'd like to, work to reduce your portion sizes.

True or false? Regular exercise may help lower your risk for heart disease.

ANSWER: True. Not only does regular exercise help you achieve or maintain a healthy body weight, it can also increase HDL (the "good" cholesterol) levels. Even better news is that you don't have to follow the "no pain, no gain" philosophy of physical activity. Recent research indicates that moderate exercise, such as walking, biking and even housekeeping, can positively affect your health.

Or if regular exercise is a problem for you, focus on increasing your activity level, thereby burning up those extra calories.

Deciding to make changes, whether in your diet, your level of physical activity or your outlook on life, is the easy part. Sticking with the changes is the challenge.

You can do it; here's how:

- Decide what is important to you in terms of your health.

- Determine what *you* can do, what steps you can take to stay well.

- Break those steps into reasonable chunks. For example, if you choose to get your cholesterol level into the healthy range and part of your plan to get there is to eat less high-fat snack foods, then come up with realistic strategies for avoiding chips and high-fat crackers. You may choose to always have a piece of fruit handy at 2 P.M. in the afternoon.

- Check your progress regularly, then make adjustments as needed.

- Stay true to your goal even when your behavior is less than perfect. It happens, and it's okay.

Recognize your successes, and reward yourself for your stick-to-itiveness. Best wishes for good health!

nutrition criteria for flags

Every recipe in this book meets at least one of the fat or cholesterol nutrition criteria described below, and most meet both fat and cholesterol criteria. Most recipes meet the low-calorie criteria, as well. The nutrition information that accompanies each recipe, along with the special nutrition criteria flags and Diet Exchanges, will help you make healthy food choices. It is unrealistic to expect each dish or even each meal to meet all nutrition guidelines. What's important is to look at total fat, cholesterol and calorie intake over an entire day. This chapter and the recipes that follow give you the information you need and the food you love to put together a healthy eating plan for yourself and your family.

LOW FAT

Main-dish recipes have 10 or fewer grams of fat per serving. Low-fat side dishes and desserts have 3 or fewer grams of fat per serving.

LOW CHOLESTEROL

Recipes have 90 or fewer milligrams of cholesterol per serving.

LOW CALORIE

Recipes have 350 or fewer calories per serving with the exception of desserts. Low-calorie desserts have 250 or fewer calories per serving.

low fat

Main-dish recipes have 10 or fewer grams of fat per serving.
Low-fat side dishes and desserts have 3 or fewer grams of fat per serving.

low cholesterol

Recipes have 90 or fewer milligrams of cholesterol per serving.

low calorie

Recipes have 350 or fewer calories per serving with the exception of desserts.
Low-calorie desserts have 250 or fewer calories per serving.

CHAPTER 1

appetizers & snacks

Smoked Salmon Pinwheels (page 41)

chipotle–black bean dip

LOW FAT / LOW CHOLESTEROL / LOW CALORIE

PREP: 20 min **BAKE:** 15 min
15 SERVINGS (2 tablespoons each)

Take a jalapeño chili, dry it and smoke it, and you end up with a wrinkly, dark-skinned chili known as chipotle. These chilies have a smoky, sweet flavor that is great in dips and sauces. In addition to dried, chipotle chilies can be found canned in adobo sauce.

2 large dried chipotle chilies

1 cup thick-and-chunky salsa

1/2 cup jalapeño-flavor black bean dip

2 tablespoons chopped fresh cilantro

1 cup shredded Colby–Monterey Jack cheese (4 ounces)

2 medium green onions, chopped (2 tablespoons)

Sweet red cherry chili half, if desired

Reduced-fat tortilla chips or Baked Tortilla Chips (page 42), if desired

Heat oven to 350°. Cover chilies with boiling water; let stand 10 minutes. Drain chilies and remove seeds. Chop chilies.

Mix chilies, salsa and bean dip. Stir in cilantro. Spoon into ungreased shallow 1-quart ovenproof serving dish. Sprinkle with cheese and onions.

Bake about 15 minutes or until mixture is hot and cheese is melted. Garnish with chili half. Serve with tortilla chips.

NUTRITION INFORMATION
1 Serving

Calories 45 (Calories from Fat 30)
Fat 3g (Saturated 2g)
Cholesterol 10mg
Sodium 150mg
Carbohydrate 2g (Dietary Fiber 1g)
Protein 2g

% DAILY VALUE: Vitamin A 6%; Vitamin C 2%; Calcium 6%; Iron 2%

DIET EXCHANGES: 1 Vegetable, 1/2 Fat

Chipotle–Black Bean Dip

hot crab-artichoke dip

LOW FAT / LOW CHOLESTEROL / LOW CALORIE

PREP: 15 min **BAKE:** 25 min
15 SERVINGS (2 tablespoons each)

1/3 cup plain fat-free yogurt

3 tablespoons reduced-fat mayonnaise

1/4 cup grated Parmesan cheese

2 cloves garlic, finely chopped

6 ounces imitation crabmeat, chopped

1 can (14 ounces) artichoke hearts, drained and coarsely chopped

1 can (4 ounces) chopped green chilies, drained

Dash of paprika

Crackers or cocktail rye bread, if desired

Heat oven to 350°. Spray 1-quart casserole with cooking spray. Mix yogurt, mayonnaise, cheese and garlic in medium bowl. Stir in crabmeat, artichoke hearts and chilies. Spoon into casserole.

Bake uncovered about 25 minutes or until golden brown and bubbly. Sprinkle with paprika before serving. Serve with crackers.

NUTRITION INFORMATION
1 Serving

Calories 40 (Calories from Fat 20)
Fat 2g (Saturated 0g)
Cholesterol 10mg
Sodium 230mg
Carbohydrate 4g (Dietary Fiber 2g)
Protein 4g

% DAILY VALUE: Vitamin A 0%; Vitamin C 6%; Calcium 4%; Iron 2%

DIET EXCHANGES: 1 Vegetable

cheesy ranch potato skins

LOW FAT / LOW CHOLESTEROL / LOW CALORIE

PREP: 10 min **BROIL:** 5 1/2 min
4 SERVINGS (2 potato skins each)

To enjoy these crispy skins in just minutes, start with leftover baked potatoes or bake the potatoes in your microwave oven. For a change of pace, top off these taters with black beans and salsa instead of the chicken, cheese and bacon.

2 medium unpeeled baking potatoes, baked*

Butter-flavored cooking spray

1/2 teaspoon garlic powder

1/4 cup finely chopped cooked chicken or turkey

1/4 cup shredded reduced-fat Cheddar cheese

2 tablespoons imitation bacon-flavor bits

Reduced-calorie ranch dressing, if desired

Cut potatoes lengthwise into fourths. Carefully scoop out pulp, leaving 1/4-inch shells. Cover and refrigerate potato pulp for another use.

Set oven control to broil. Place potato shells, skin sides down, on rack in broiler pan. Spray with cooking spray. Sprinkle with garlic powder. Broil with tops 4 to 5 inches from heat about 5 minutes or until crisp and brown.

Sprinkle chicken and cheese over potato shells. Broil about 30 seconds or until cheese is melted. Sprinkle with bacon bits. Serve hot with ranch dressing.

*To "bake" potatoes in microwave oven, pierce potatoes with fork. Arrange potatoes about 1 inch apart in circle on microwavable paper towel. Microwave uncovered on High 8 to 10 minutes or until tender. To bake potatoes in conventional oven, pierce potatoes with fork. Bake in 375° oven 1 to 1 1/2 hours or until tender. Let potatoes stand until cool enough to handle.

NUTRITION INFORMATION
1 Serving

Calories 105 (Calories from Fat 20)
Fat 2g (Saturated 1g)
Cholesterol 10mg
Sodium 120mg
Carbohydrate 17g (Dietary Fiber 2g)
Protein 7g

% DAILY VALUE: Vitamin A 0%; Vitamin C 6%; Calcium 4%; Iron 6%

DIET EXCHANGES: 1 Starch, 1/2 Lean Meat

zippy chicken drummies

LOW FAT / LOW CHOLESTEROL / LOW CALORIE

PREP: 30 min **MARINATE:** 15 min **BAKE:** 30 min
12 SERVINGS (2 drummies and 1 tablespoon sauce each)

2 pounds chicken drummettes (about 24)

2 tablespoons honey

2 tablespoons ketchup

2 teaspoons red pepper sauce

1 tablespoon Worcestershire sauce

Blue Cheese Dipping Sauce (below)

Celery sticks, if desired

Remove skin and fat from chicken. Mix honey, ketchup, pepper sauce, and Worcestershire sauce in heavy-duty resealable plastic food-storage bag. Add chicken; turn to coat with honey mixture. Seal bag and refrigerate at least 15 minutes but no longer than 24 hours, turning occasionally. Make Blue Cheese Dipping Sauce.

Heat oven to 350°. Line jelly roll pan, 15 1/2 × 10 1/2 × 1 inch, with aluminum foil. Place chicken in pan. Bake uncovered about 30 minutes or until crisp and juice of chicken is no longer pink when centers of thickest pieces are cut. Serve with Blue Cheese Dipping Sauce and celery sticks.

Blue Cheese Dipping Sauce

1/3 cup fat-free small curd cottage cheese

1/2 teaspoon white wine vinegar

2 tablespoons fat-free (skim) milk

1/8 teaspoon white pepper

1 clove garlic, finely chopped

1 tablespoon crumbled blue cheese

Place cottage cheese, vinegar, milk, white pepper, garlic and half of the blue cheese in blender or food processor. Cover and blend on low speed until smooth and creamy. Spoon into serving dish. Stir in remaining blue cheese. Cover and refrigerate until serving.

NUTRITION INFORMATION
1 Serving

Calories 60 (Calories from Fat 20)
Fat 2g (Saturated 1g)
Cholesterol 15mg
Sodium 150mg
Carbohydrate 4g (Dietary Fiber 0g)
Protein 6g

% DAILY VALUE: Vitamin A 0%; Vitamin C 2%; Calcium 0%; Iron 2%

DIET EXCHANGES: 1 Lean Meat

Zippy Chicken Drummies

maple-glazed BBQ meatballs

LOW FAT / LOW CHOLESTEROL / LOW CALORIE

PREP: 25 min **BAKE:** 20 min
About **3 DOZEN** appetizers

These meaty morsels pack a mouthful of smoky maple flavor! If Mexican food is your passion, you may want to substitute tomato sauce in place of the barbecue sauce and salsa instead of the syrup. Toss in some chopped jalapeño chilies, and you'll really turn up the heat!

1 pound ground turkey breast

2 egg whites

1 small onion, finely chopped (1/4 cup)

1/2 cup dry bread crumbs

1/4 cup fat-free (skim) milk

1 teaspoon salt

1/4 teaspoon pepper

3/4 cup barbecue sauce

1/4 cup maple-flavored syrup

Heat oven to 400°. Spray rectangular pan, 13 × 9 × 2 inches, with cooking spray. Mix turkey, egg whites, onion, bread crumbs, milk, salt and pepper. Shape mixture into 1-inch balls. Arrange meatballs, sides not touching, in pan.

Bake uncovered 15 to 20 minutes or until turkey is no longer pink. Heat barbecue sauce and syrup in 1-quart saucepan, stirring occasionally, until hot.

Place meatballs in chafing dish or serving dish. Pour sauce mixture over meatballs, or serve it on the side for dipping.

NUTRITION INFORMATION
1 Appetizer

Calories 35 (Calories from Fat 10)
Fat 1g (Saturated 0g)
Cholesterol 10mg
Sodium 135mg
Carbohydrate 4g (Dietary Fiber 0g)
Protein 3g

% DAILY VALUE: Vitamin A 0%; Vitamin C 0%; Calcium 0%; Iron 0%

DIET EXCHANGES: 1/2 Very Lean Meat, 1/2 Vegetable

tomato bruschetta with basil spread

LOW FAT / LOW CHOLESTEROL / LOW CALORIE

PREP: 15 min **BROIL:** 3 min
12 APPETIZERS

12 slices French bread, 1/2 inch thick

1/2 package (8-ounce size) reduced-fat cream cheese (Neufchâtel), softened

1 tablespoon chopped fresh or 1 teaspoon dried basil or oregano leaves

1 small tomato, chopped (1/2 cup)

1 medium green onion, sliced (1 tablespoon)

1 tablespoon chopped ripe olives

Set oven control to broil. Place bread slices on cookie sheet. Broil with tops 3 to 4 inches from heat 1 to 2 minutes or until lightly toasted.

Mix cream cheese and basil; spread on untoasted sides of bread slices. Broil about 1 minute or until cheese mixture is melted. Top with tomato, onion and olives.

NUTRITION INFORMATION
1 Appetizer

Calories 90 (Calories from Fat 25)
Fat 3g (Saturated 2g)
Cholesterol 10mg
Sodium 190mg
Carbohydrate 14g (Dietary Fiber 1g)
Protein 0g

% DAILY VALUE: Vitamin A 4%; Vitamin C 4%; Calcium 4%; Iron 4%

DIET EXCHANGES: 1 Starch, 1/2 Fat

vegetable pot stickers

LOW FAT / LOW CHOLESTEROL / LOW CALORIE

PREP: 35 min **COOK:** 10 min
10 SERVINGS (3 pot stickers each)

If you love making pot stickers and other dumplings, you may want to purchase a dumpling maker. These gadgets make quick work of filling, folding and crimping. Look for them at kitchenware stores or in the kitchen-gadget section of a department store.

1 1/2 cups fat-free chicken broth

1 medium onion, finely chopped (1/2 cup)

1 medium stalk celery, finely chopped (1/2 cup)

1/2 cup thinly sliced cabbage

1/2 cup chopped mushrooms

1 teaspoon grated gingerroot

2 cloves garlic, finely chopped

1 teaspoon soy sauce

1 teaspoon dark sesame oil

1/2 package (16-ounce size) wonton skins (30 skins)

Heat 3/4 cup of the broth to boiling in 10-inch nonstick skillet over medium-high heat. Stir in onion, celery, cabbage, mushrooms, gingerroot, and garlic. Cook 5 to 8 minutes, stirring frequently and adding more broth if vegetables begin to stick, until vegetables are tender; remove from heat. Stir in soy sauce and sesame oil. Remove vegetable mixture from skillet. Wipe out skillet.

Brush edges of 1 wonton skin with water. Place 1 heaping teaspoon vegetable mixture on center of skin. Fold skin in half over filling and pinch edges to seal. Make creases in sealed edges to form pleats on one side of each pot sticker. Repeat with remaining wonton skins and vegetable mixture.

Spray skillet with cooking spray; heat skillet over medium heat. Cook pot stickers in skillet, pleated sides up, about 1 minute or until bottoms are light brown. Add remaining 3/4 cup broth. Cover and cook 5 to 8 minutes or until most of liquid is absorbed.

NUTRITION INFORMATION
1 Serving

Calories 25 (Calories from Fat 0)
Fat 0g (Saturated 0g)
Cholesterol 5mg
Sodium 70mg
Carbohydrate 5g (Dietary Fiber 0g)
Protein 1g

% DAILY VALUE: Vitamin A 0%; Vitamin C 0%; Calcium 0%; Iron 2%

DIET EXCHANGES: 1 Vegetable

Vegetable Pot Stickers

chewy pizza bread

LOW FAT / LOW CHOLESTEROL / LOW CALORIE

PREP: 10 min **BAKE:** 20 min
8 SERVINGS (2 squares each)

1 1/2 cups all-purpose flour

1 1/2 teaspoons baking powder

1/2 teaspoon salt

3/4 cup regular or nonalcoholic beer

1/2 cup spaghetti sauce

1/3 cup shredded low-fat mozzarella cheese

Chopped fresh basil leaves, if desired

Heat oven to 425°. Spray square pan, 8 × 8 × 2 inches, with cooking spray. Mix flour, baking powder and salt in medium bowl. Stir in beer just until flour is moistened. Spread dough in pan. Spread spaghetti sauce over dough. Sprinkle with cheese.

Bake 15 to 20 minutes or until toothpick inserted in center comes out clean. Sprinkle with basil. Cut into 2-inch squares. Serve warm.

NUTRITION INFORMATION
1 Serving

Calories 120 (Calories from Fat 20)
Fat 2g (Saturated 1g)
Cholesterol 5mg
Sodium 200mg
Carbohydrate 22g (Dietary Fiber 1g)
Protein 4g

% DAILY VALUE: Vitamin A 2%; Vitamin C 2%; Calcium 8%; Iron 6%

DIET EXCHANGES: 2 1/2 Starch

Chewy Pizza Bread

parmesan puffs with marinara

PREP: 20 min **BAKE:** 15 min
30 APPETIZERS

These mini puffs are a perfect party finger food. You can even prepare them days or weeks before the big day. Simply bake and cool puffs, then wrap tightly and freeze. When ready to serve, place puffs in muffin cups and pop them in a 350° oven 8 to 10 minutes or until hot.

1/2 cup fat-free (skim) milk

1/4 cup margarine

1/2 cup all-purpose flour

2 eggs

3/4 cup grated Parmesan cheese

1 cup marinara sauce, heated

Heat oven to 375°. Grease cookie sheet. Heat milk and margarine to boiling in 1 1/2-quart saucepan. Stir in flour; reduce heat to low. Stir vigorously about 1 minute or until mixture forms a ball; remove from heat.

Beat in eggs, one at a time, beating until smooth after each addition. Stir in cheese. Drop dough by rounded teaspoonfuls 2 inches apart onto cookie sheet.

Bake about 15 minutes or until puffed and golden brown. Serve warm with marinara sauce for dipping.

NUTRITION INFORMATION
1 Appetizer

Calories 45 (Calories from Fat 25)
Fat 3g (Saturated 1g)
Cholesterol 15mg
Sodium 105mg
Carbohydrate 3g (Dietary Fiber 0g)
Protein 2g

% DAILY VALUE: Vitamin A 4%; Vitamin C 0%; Calcium 4%; Iron 0%

DIET EXCHANGES: 1 Fat

smoked salmon pinwheels

LOW FAT / LOW CHOLESTEROL / LOW CALORIE

PREP: 15 min **CHILL:** 2 hr
24 APPETIZERS

The holidays don't have to mean high fat, especially when you have these festive spirals gracing your party platter. Green spinach and red bell pepper team up for a colorful combination; but if you prefer, try out some other veggie combinations such as shredded carrots, finely chopped cucumbers, or chopped roma (plum) tomatoes.

1 package (8 ounces) reduced-fat cream cheese (Neufchâtel), softened

1 tablespoon chopped fresh or 1 teaspoon dried dill weed

4 flour tortillas (10 inches in diameter)

1 package (4 1/2 ounces) smoked salmon, skinned and finely chopped

12 to 16 leaves fresh spinach

16 strips red bell pepper, about 5 × 1/4 inch

Mix cream cheese and dill weed. Spread about 1/4 cup of the cream cheese mixture over each tortilla. Sprinkle each with 1/4 cup salmon. Place 3 or 4 spinach leaves and 4 bell pepper strips evenly spaced on each tortilla.

Roll up tortillas tightly, spreading with additional cream cheese mixture to seal roll. Wrap securely with plastic wrap and refrigerate at least 2 hours but no longer than 24 hours.

To serve, cut tortilla rolls into 1-inch pieces. Place cut side up on serving platter.

NUTRITION INFORMATION
1 Appetizer

Calories 65 (Calories from Fat 25)
Fat 3g (Saturated 2g)
Cholesterol 10mg
Sodium 130mg
Carbohydrate 7g (Dietary Fiber 1g)
Protein 3g%

DAILY VALUE: Vitamin A 10%; Vitamin C 10%; Calcium 2%; Iron 4%

DIET EXCHANGES: 1/2 Starch, 1/2 Fat

baked tortilla chips

LOW FAT / LOW CHOLESTEROL / LOW CALORIE

PREP: 5 min **BAKE:** 6 min
8 SERVINGS (8 chips each)

8 yellow or blue corn tortillas (5 or 6 inches in diameter)

Heat oven to 450°. Spray 2 cookie sheets with cooking spray. Cut each tortilla into 8 wedges. Place in single layer on cookie sheets.

Bake about 6 minutes or until crisp but not brown; cool. Store in airtight container at room temperature.

NUTRITION INFORMATION
1 Serving

Calories 50 (Calories from Fat 10)
Fat 1g (Saturated 0g)
Cholesterol 0mg
Sodium 35mg
Carbohydrate 10g (Dietary Fiber 1g)
Protein 1g

% DAILY VALUE: Vitamin A 0%; Vitamin C 0%; Calcium 4%; Iron 2%

DIET EXCHANGES: 1/2 Starch

Baked Tortilla Chips and Fresh Garden Salsa (page 44)

fresh garden salsa

LOW FAT / LOW CHOLESTEROL / LOW CALORIE

PREP: 15 min
8 SERVINGS (1/4 cup each)

If you love the combination of sweet and hot, add 1/2 cup chopped pineapple, peaches or mango for a dynamite fire-and-ice fruit salsa.

1 large tomato, finely chopped (1 cup)

1 small green bell pepper, finely chopped (3/4 cup)

1/2 cup finely chopped unpeeled cucumber

1/4 cup finely chopped radishes or red onion

3 tablespoons chopped fresh cilantro or parsley

1 tablespoon lime juice

1 1/2 teaspoons cider vinegar

1/4 teaspoon salt

1 jalapeño chili, seeded and finely chopped

Mix all ingredients in glass or plastic bowl. Cover and refrigerate until serving.

NUTRITION INFORMATION
1 Serving

Calories 10 (Calories from Fat 0)
Fat 0g (Saturated 0g)
Cholesterol 0mg
Sodium 5mg
Carbohydrate 3g (Dietary Fiber 1g)
Protein 0g

% DAILY VALUE: Vitamin A 8%; Vitamin C 42%; Calcium 0%; Iron 0%

DIET EXCHANGES: 1 Serving free

savory popcorn mix

LOW CHOLESTEROL / LOW CALORIE

PREP: 10 min **BAKE:** 30 min
8 SERVINGS (1 cup each)

If you don't have a hot-air popcorn popper, purchase popped popcorn at the supermarket. Just be sure to select a "light" type.

6 cups hot-air-popped popcorn

2 cups fat-free pretzel sticks

1 cup tiny fish-shaped crackers

2 tablespoons margarine, melted

1/2 teaspoon garlic powder

1/2 teaspoon onion powder

1/2 teaspoon dried basil leaves

1/2 teaspoon dried oregano leaves

1/8 teaspoon red pepper sauce

Heat oven to 300°. Mix popcorn, pretzels and crackers in ungreased rectangular pan, 13 × 9 × 2 inches. Mix remaining ingredients; drizzle over popcorn mixture. Toss until evenly coated.

Bake about 30 minutes, stirring every 10 minutes, until toasted. Serve warm. Store in airtight container at room temperature.

NUTRITION INFORMATION
1 Serving

Calories 120 (Calories from Fat 45)
Fat 5g (Saturated 1g)
Cholesterol 0mg
Sodium 300mg
Carbohydrate 19g (Dietary Fiber 2g)
Protein 2g

% DAILY VALUE: Vitamin A 4%; Vitamin C 0%; Calcium 0%; Iron 4%

DIET EXCHANGES: 1 Starch, 1 Fat

honey-spice pretzels

LOW FAT / LOW CHOLESTEROL / LOW CALORIE

PREP: 10 min **BAKE:** 8 min
4 SERVINGS (1 cup each)

4 cups fat-free pretzel sticks

3 tablespoons honey

1 teaspoon onion powder

1 teaspoon chili powder

2 teaspoons margarine, melted

Heat oven to 350°. Line cookie sheet with aluminum foil; spray with cooking spray. Place pretzels in large bowl. Mix remaining ingredients; drizzle over pretzels. Toss until evenly coated. Spread pretzels evenly on cookie sheet.

Bake 8 minutes, stirring once. Cool on cookie sheet. Loosen pretzels from foil. Store in airtight container at room temperature.

NUTRITION INFORMATION
1 Serving

Calories 225 (Calories from Fat 20)
Fat 2g (Saturated 1g)
Cholesterol 0mg
Sodium 800mg
Carbohydrate 50g (Dietary Fiber 2g)
Protein 4g

% DAILY VALUE: Vitamin A 4%; Vitamin C 0%; Calcium 2%; Iron 12%

DIET EXCHANGES: 3 Starch

THE SNACK ATTACK

The "three squares a day" crowd is getting trampled by grazers. More and more people, especially kids and teenagers, are snacking. That can be a good thing. Snacking is a great way to fuel your body throughout the day with mini-meals and avoid binge eating later on. Here's how:

- Stock the pantry and refrigerator with healthy foods. If the chips and dip aren't there, they're out of sight and, hopefully, out of mind.

- Watch portion amounts. Instead of eating crackers, popcorn and other munchies directly out of the bag, pour a certain amount into a separate container. Pay attention to eating while you're eating. If you snack mindlessly while watching TV or doing some other activity, it's easy to overeat.

- Take a look at your overall diet, comparing it with what experts recommend you "should have" for good health. Are you low in fruits, vegetables, whole grains? Slip whichever foods you're lacking into your snacking plan.

Snack Suggestions

Many snacks fall into two categories: chips or candy. Here are some options for that standard fare:

Instead of	Try	Benefits
Potato Chips (snack-pack size)	Whole grain ready-to-eat cereal mixed with dried fruit	Save 10 grams of fat plus get a good dose of fiber and lots of vitamins and minerals.
	Baked tortilla chips with salsa	Vitamin C, potassium and lycopenes (cancer-preventing substances found in tomatoes)
	Breadsticks and string cheese	Calcium and protein
Candy bar (regular size)	Fat-free yogurt (any flavor) with fruit and a few chocolate chips	Save at least 10 grams of fat plus get one-fourth of your daily calcium needs plus other nutrients and fiber.
	Ready-to-eat pudding	Calcium and potassium
	Applesauce with animal crackers or fat-free vanilla wafers	Save at least 10 grams of fat.

low fat

Main-dish recipes have 10 or fewer grams of fat per serving.
Low-fat side dishes and desserts have 3 or fewer grams of fat per serving.

low cholesterol

Recipes have 90 or fewer milligrams of cholesterol per serving.

low calorie

Recipes have 350 or fewer calories per serving with the exception of desserts.
Low-calorie desserts have 250 or fewer calories per serving.

CHAPTER 2

poultry, fish & seafood

Spicy Chicken Drumsticks (page 62)

hot seared chicken

LOW FAT / LOW CHOLESTEROL / LOW CALORIE

PREP: 10 min **COOK:** 10 min
4 SERVINGS

Cumin plays a double role in this dish. Not only does it offer a spicy bite of its own, it also highlights all of the other delicious flavors in this quick-to-fix meal.

4 boneless, skinless chicken breast halves (about 1 1/4 pounds)

1 tablespoon lime juice

1 1/2 teaspoons blackened seasoning mixture or jerk seasoning (dry)

1/8 teaspoon ground cumin

2 teaspoons margarine

1/4 cup water

Hot cooked couscous, if desired

Remove fat from chicken. Mix 1 1/2 teaspoons of the lime juice, the seasoning mixture and cumin. Rub mixture evenly over both sides of chicken.

Spray 10-inch nonstick skillet with cooking spray; heat over medium-high heat. Melt margarine in skillet. Cook chicken in margarine about 8 minutes, turning once, until chicken is no longer pink when centers of thickest pieces are cut. Remove chicken from skillet; keep warm.

Add remaining 1 1/2 teaspoons lime juice and the water to drippings in skillet. Heat to boiling. Boil and stir about 45 seconds or until liquid is reduced to about 2 tablespoons. Spoon sauce over chicken. Serve with couscous.

NUTRITION INFORMATION
1 Serving

Calories 165 (Calories from Fat 55)
Fat 6g (Saturated 1g)
Cholesterol 75mg
Sodium 90mg
Carbohydrate 1g (Dietary Fiber 0g)
Protein 27g

% DAILY VALUE: Vitamin A 2%; Vitamin C 0%; Calcium 2%; Iron 6%

DIET EXCHANGES: 4 Very Lean Meat, 1/2 Fat

Hot Seared Chicken

provençal lemon chicken

LOW FAT / LOW CHOLESTEROL / LOW CALORIE

PREP: 10 min **COOK:** 15 min
4 SERVINGS

4 boneless, skinless chicken breast halves (about 1 1/4 pounds)

2 tablespoons chopped fresh or 2 teaspoons dried basil leaves

2 tablespoons chopped fresh parsley

2 tablespoons lemon juice

2 teaspoons olive or vegetable oil

1/2 teaspoon salt

1 clove garlic, finely chopped

Remove fat from chicken. Beat remaining ingredients with wire whisk until blended.

Spray 10-inch nonstick skillet with cooking spray; heat over medium-high heat. Cook chicken in skillet about 15 minutes, turning once, until juice of chicken is no longer pink when centers of thickest pieces are cut.

Spoon lemon sauce over chicken. Turn chicken and cook 15 seconds longer. Serve chicken topped with sauce. Sprinkle with additional chopped fresh parsley if desired.

NUTRITION INFORMATION
1 Serving

Calories 160 (Calories from Fat 55)
Fat 6g (Saturated 1g)
Cholesterol 75mg
Sodium 70mg
Carbohydrate 0g (Dietary Fiber 0g)
Protein 27g

% DAILY VALUE: Vitamin A 0%; Vitamin C 0%; Calcium 0%; Iron 4%

DIET EXCHANGES: 4 Very Lean Meat

baked oregano chicken

LOW FAT / LOW CHOLESTEROL / LOW CALORIE

PREP: 10 min **BAKE:** 25 min
4 SERVINGS

4 boneless, skinless chicken breast halves (about 1 1/4 pounds)

1/4 cup dry bread crumbs

2 tablespoons grated Parmesan cheese

1/4 teaspoon dried oregano leaves

1/8 teaspoon garlic salt

1/8 teaspoon pepper

1/4 cup Dijon mustard

Heat oven to 425°. Spray square pan, 9 × 9 × 2 inches, with cooking spray. Remove fat from chicken.

Mix bread crumbs, cheese, oregano, garlic salt and pepper. Spread mustard on all sides of chicken. Coat chicken with bread crumb mixture. Place in pan.

Bake uncovered about 25 minutes or until juice of chicken is no longer pink when centers of thickest pieces are cut.

NUTRITION INFORMATION
1 Serving

Calories 210 (Calories from Fat 55)
Fat 6g (Saturated 2g)
Cholesterol 85mg
Sodium 450mg
Carbohydrate 6g (Dietary Fiber 1g)
Protein 34g

% DAILY VALUE: Vitamin A 0%; Vitamin C 0%; Calcium 8%; Iron 10%

DIET EXCHANGES: 1 Starch, 4 1/2 Very Lean Meat

THE PARTICULARS ON POULTRY

Poultry can be a boon or a bust to a low-fat diet, depending on how it is prepared. Take a look at the big differences among baked and fried.

Food	Fat (g)	Saturated Fat (g)	Cholesterol (mg)
CHICKEN (3 OUNCES, COOKED)			
Light meat, skinless, baked	4	1.0	75
Light meat, with skin, baked	9	2.5	75
Dark meat, skinless, baked	8	2.0	80
Dark meat, with skin, baked	13	5.5	80
Light meat, skinless, fried	5	1.5	75
Light meat, with skin, fried	10	3.0	75
Nuggets, battered, fried	16	3.5	60
TURKEY (3 OUNCES, COOKED)			
Light meat, skinless, baked	2.5	<1	60
Light meat, with skin, baked	7	2.0	65
Dark meat, skinless, baked	7	2.0	75
Dark meat, with skin, baked	9.5	3.0	75

oven-fried chicken nuggets

LOW FAT / LOW CHOLESTEROL / LOW CALORIE

PREP: 20 min **BAKE:** 30 min

6 SERVINGS

Fast food without the fat! You won't believe these tasty chicken bites are baked, not fried, in a cornflake crust. In addition to the two dipping sauces we suggest below, try honey or low-fat ranch dressing.

2 pounds boneless, skinless chicken breast halves

3/4 cup cornflakes cereal

1/2 cup all-purpose flour

3/4 teaspoon salt

1/2 teaspoon paprika

1/2 teaspoon pepper

1/3 cup buttermilk

Cooking spray

1/2 cup barbecue sauce

1/2 cup sweet-and-sour sauce

Heat oven to 400°. Line jelly roll pan, 15 1/2 × 10 1/2 × 1 inch, with aluminum foil. Remove fat from chicken. Cut chicken into 2-inch pieces.

Place cereal, flour, salt, paprika and pepper in blender. Cover and blend on medium speed until cereal is reduced to crumbs; pour into bowl.

Place chicken and buttermilk in heavy-duty resealable plastic food-storage bag. Seal bag and let stand 5 minutes, turning once. Dip chicken into cereal mixture to coat. Place in pan. Spray chicken with cooking spray.

Bake uncovered about 30 minutes or until crisp and chicken is no longer pink in center. Serve with barbecue sauce and sweet-and-sour sauce.

NUTRITION INFORMATION
1 Serving

Calories 270 (Calories from Fat 55)
Fat 6g (Saturated 2g)
Cholesterol 90mg
Sodium 670mg
Carbohydrate 20g (Dietary Fiber 1g)
Protein 35g

% DAILY VALUE: Vitamin A 6%; Vitamin C 2%; Calcium 4%; Iron 16%

DIET EXCHANGES: 1 Starch, 4 Very Lean Meat, 1 Vegetable

Oven-Fried Chicken Nuggets

summer garden chicken stir-fry

LOW FAT / LOW CHOLESTEROL / LOW CALORIE

PREP: 15 min **COOK:** 15 min
4 SERVINGS

Scurrying to get dinner on the table? Make it easy—use 4 to 5 cups of your favorite fresh vegetables from the salad bar for the vegetable combination in this recipe. Or substitute a 16-ounce bag of precut stir-fry vegetables available in the produce section of your supermarket.

1 pound boneless, skinless chicken breast halves

2 cloves garlic, finely chopped

2 teaspoons finely chopped gingerroot

1 medium onion, cut into thin wedges

1 cup baby-cut carrots, cut lengthwise in half

1 cup fat-free chicken broth

3 tablespoons reduced-sodium soy sauce

2 to 3 teaspoons sugar

2 cups broccoli flowerets

1 cup sliced mushrooms (3 ounces)

1/2 cup chopped red bell pepper

2 teaspoons cornstarch

Hot cooked rice, if desired

Remove fat from chicken. Cut chicken into 1-inch pieces. Spray 12-inch nonstick skillet with cooking spray; heat over medium-high heat. Add chicken, garlic and gingerroot; stir-fry 2 to 3 minutes or until chicken is brown.

Add onion, carrots, 3/4 cup of the broth, the soy sauce and sugar. Cover and cook over medium heat 5 minutes, stirring occasionally.

Add broccoli, mushrooms and bell pepper. Cover and cook about 5 minutes, stirring occasionally, until chicken is no longer pink in center and vegetables are crisp-tender.

Mix cornstarch and remaining 1/4 cup broth; stir into chicken mixture. Cook, stirring frequently, until sauce is thickened. Serve over rice.

NUTRITION INFORMATION
1 Serving

Calories 200 (Calories from Fat 35)
Fat 4g (Saturated 1g)
Cholesterol 70mg
Sodium 600mg
Carbohydrate 15g (Dietary Fiber 3g)
Protein 29g

% DAILY VALUE: Vitamin A 52%; Vitamin C 46%; Calcium 4%; Iron 12%

DIET EXCHANGES: 3 1/2 Very Lean Meat, 3 Vegetable

risotto-style gorgonzola chicken & orzo

LOW FAT / LOW CHOLESTEROL / LOW CALORIE

PREP: 10 min **COOK:** 20 min
6 SERVINGS

Hot stock, Arborio rice, and lots of stirring make up the traditional recipe for the rich and creamy concoction known as risotto. In this enlightened version, we've cut the fat and the labor for an equally mouthwatering meal. Gorgonzola adds a tangy richness to this dish, but you can use grated Parmesan cheese if you prefer a milder flavor.

1 1/2 pounds boneless, skinless chicken breast halves

1 large onion, finely chopped (1 cup)

1 can (14 1/2 ounces) ready-to-serve fat-free chicken broth

1 1/2 cups uncooked rosamarina (orzo) pasta (9 ounces)

3/4 teaspoon Italian seasoning

1/2 teaspoon lemon pepper

1/3 cup crumbled Gorgonzola cheese

Remove fat from chicken. Cut chicken into 1/2-inch strips. Spray 10-inch nonstick skillet with cooking spray; heat over medium-high heat. Cook chicken in skillet about 2 minutes, stirring frequently, until brown. Remove chicken from skillet; keep warm.

Spray skillet with cooking spray. Cook onion in skillet over medium-high heat about 4 minutes, stirring frequently, until tender. Stir in broth, pasta, Italian seasoning, lemon pepper and chicken. Heat to boiling; reduce heat to low. Simmer uncovered about 11 minutes, stirring occasionally, until pasta is just tender; remove from heat. Stir in cheese.

NUTRITION INFORMATION
1 Serving

Calories 240 (Calories from Fat 35)
Fat 4g (Saturated 1g)
Cholesterol 40mg
Sodium 430mg
Carbohydrate 32g (Dietary Fiber 2g)
Protein 21g

% DAILY VALUE: Vitamin A 0%; Vitamin C 0%; Calcium 6%; Iron 12%

DIET EXCHANGES: 2 Starch, 2 Lean Meat

southwest chicken & chili stew

LOW FAT / LOW CHOLESTEROL / LOW CALORIE

PREP: 15 min **COOK:** 30 min
4 SERVINGS

1 pound boneless, skinless chicken breast halves or thighs

2 1/4 cups fat-free chicken broth

4 cloves garlic, finely chopped

1 to 2 medium jalapeño chilies, seeded and diced

2 teaspoons all-purpose flour

1 medium red bell pepper, diced (1 cup)

1 medium carrot, sliced (1/2 cup)

1 cup whole kernel corn

2 tablespoons finely chopped fresh cilantro

1/4 teaspoon salt

1/4 teaspoon pepper

1/2 teaspoon ground cumin

1 teaspoon cornstarch

1/4 cup cold water

Reduced-fat tortilla chips or Baked Tortilla Chips (page 42), if desired

Remove fat from chicken. Cut chicken into 1-inch pieces. Heat 1/2 cup of the broth to boiling in 3-quart saucepan. Cook chicken in broth about 5 minutes, stirring occasionally, until white. Remove chicken from broth with slotted spoon.

Cook garlic and chilies in broth in Dutch oven over medium-high heat 2 minutes, stirring frequently. Stir in flour; reduce heat to low. Cook 2 minutes, stirring constantly. Gradually stir in remaining 1 3/4 cups broth.

Stir in chicken and remaining ingredients except cornstarch, water, and tortilla chips. Heat to boiling; reduce heat. Cover and simmer about 20 minutes, stirring occasionally, until chicken is no longer pink in center.

Mix cornstarch and water; stir into chicken mixture. Cook, stirring frequently, until heated through and thickened. Serve with tortilla chips.

NUTRITION INFORMATION
1 Serving

Calories 230 (Calories from Fat 45)
Fat 5g (Saturated 1g)
Cholesterol 70mg
Sodium 610mg
Carbohydrate 18g (Dietary Fiber 2g)
Protein 30g

% DAILY VALUE: Vitamin A 52%; Vitamin C 70%; Calcium 2%; Iron 12%

DIET EXCHANGES: 1 Starch, 4 Very Lean Meat

Southwest Chicken & Chili Stew

border chicken & bean soup

LOW FAT / LOW CHOLESTEROL / LOW CALORIE

PREP: 10 min **COOK:** 20 min
6 SERVINGS

3/4 pound boneless, skinless chicken thighs or breast halves

3 cups fat-free reduced-sodium chicken broth

1 can (14 1/2 ounces) no-salt-added diced tomatoes, undrained

1 envelope (1 1/4 ounces) taco seasoning mix

1 can (15 to 16 ounces) navy beans, rinsed and drained

1 1/2 teaspoons sugar

Remove fat from chicken. Cut chicken into 1/2-inch pieces. Spray 4-quart Dutch oven with cooking spray; heat over medium-high heat. Cook chicken in Dutch oven about 3 minutes, stirring frequently, until brown.

Stir in remaining ingredients. Heat to boiling; reduce heat to low. Simmer uncovered about 15 minutes or until chicken is no longer pink in center.

NUTRITION INFORMATION
1 Serving

Calories 225 (Calories from Fat 55)
Fat 6g (Saturated 2g)
Cholesterol 35mg
Sodium 890mg
Carbohydrate 27g (Dietary Fiber 6g)
Protein 22g

% DAILY VALUE: Vitamin A 8%; Vitamin C 10%; Calcium 10%; Iron 20%

DIET EXCHANGES: 1 Starch, 2 Lean Meat, 2 Vegetable

LOW-FAT COOKING 101: MAKING FATLESS CHICKEN BROTH

True, canned chicken broth is convenient, but the homemade variety is far better than anything you can buy at the store. And it's easier to make than you may think. Here's how:

To make broth: Heat 10 cups water, 1 cup each chopped carrots, celery and onion, 1 teaspoon salt, 3- to 3 1/2-pound whole broiler-fryer chicken and 4 sprigs parsley to boiling in 8-quart Dutch oven. Reduce heat to low; cover and simmer 2 hours. Remove chicken from broth; cool. Remove skin and bones from chicken; reserve chicken for another use. Pour broth through a wire-mesh strainer into large bowl; discard solids. Follow one of the techniques below for removing fat from broth.

Pour It!

Keep the fat at the top of the broth with a fat separator. Using a fat separator allows fat to float to the top, so you can pour the fat-free broth into a bowl. Just be sure to stop pouring when you reach the layer of fat.

OR

Ice It!

Cool broth slightly. Place a strainer filled with ice over a bowl. Pour broth over ice. The unwanted fat will cling to the ice.

OR

Chill It!

Refrigerate cooked broth for several hours or until the fat forms a solid layer on top of the liquid. Then use a spoon or metal spatula to scrape off the fat.

spicy chicken drumsticks

LOW FAT / LOW CALORIE

PREP: 20 min **BAKE:** 45 min
4 SERVINGS

Crispy, crunchy chicken doesn't have to be deep-fried to be delicious! For a true taste of the South, serve these drumsticks with corn bread muffins drizzled with honey or warm maple syrup.

2 pounds chicken drumsticks

1/3 cup all-purpose flour

1/3 cup yellow cornmeal

1/2 teaspoon ground cumin

1/2 teaspoon chili powder

1/4 teaspoon salt

1/3 cup buttermilk

1/4 teaspoon red pepper sauce

Cooking spray

Heat oven to 400°. Spray rectangular pan, 13 × 9 × 2 inches, with cooking spray. Remove skin and fat from chicken.

Mix flour, cornmeal, cumin, chili powder and salt in heavy-duty resealable plastic food-storage bag. Mix buttermilk and pepper sauce in medium bowl. Dip chicken into buttermilk mixture, then place in bag. Seal bag and shake until evenly coated. Place in pan. Spray chicken lightly with cooking spray.

Bake uncovered 40 to 45 minutes or until juice of chicken is no longer pink when centers of thickest pieces are cut.

NUTRITION INFORMATION
1 Serving

Calories 230 (Calories from Fat 45)
Fat 5g (Saturated 2g)
Cholesterol 105mg
Sodium 240mg
Carbohydrate 18g (Dietary Fiber 1g)
Protein 29g

% DAILY VALUE: Vitamin A 0%; Vitamin C 0%; Calcium 4%; Iron 18%

DIET EXCHANGES: 1 Starch, 4 Very Lean Meat

LOW-FAT COOKING 101: TRIM THE FAT FROM CHICKEN

Here's the skinny on chicken: Most of the fat in poultry is hidden in the skin. If you eat chicken without the skin, you'll slash your fat and saturated fat intake in half!

1. Shed the Skin!

Remove the skin from chicken. Here's a handy trick: Grab the skin with a paper towel. (You can also remove the skin after the chicken is cooked to keep the flavor and moistness in—however, if the chicken is cooked with other ingredients, some of the fat will melt into the rest of the dish.)

2. Trim the Fat!

Cut any visible fat from chicken with a kitchen scissors or knife.

chicken & corn bread stuffing casserole

LOW FAT / LOW CHOLESTEROL / LOW CALORIE

PREP: 15 min **BAKE:** 15 min
4 SERVINGS

This comfy casserole is a true reminder of Thanksgiving, in just a matter of minutes. Crazy about cranberries? Try a side of cranberry sauce spiked with a little orange-flavored liqueur or orange juice and grated orange peel.

1 can (10 3/4 ounces) condensed 98% fat-free cream of chicken or celery soup

3/4 cup fat-free (skim) milk

1 package (10 ounces) frozen mixed vegetables, thawed and drained

1 medium onion, finely chopped (1/2 cup)

1/2 teaspoon ground sage or poultry seasoning

2 cups cut-up cooked chicken or turkey breast

1 1/2 cups corn bread stuffing mix

1/8 teaspoon pepper

Paprika, if desired

Heat oven to 400°. Spray 3-quart casserole with cooking spray.

Heat soup and milk to boiling in 3-quart saucepan over high heat, stirring frequently. Stir in mixed vegetables, onion and sage. Heat to boiling, stirring frequently; remove from heat.

Stir in chicken and stuffing mix. Spoon into casserole. Sprinkle with pepper and paprika. Bake uncovered about 15 minutes or until hot in center.

NUTRITION INFORMATION
1 Serving

Calories 285 (Calories from Fat 55)
Fat 6g (Saturated 2g)
Cholesterol 60mg
Sodium 1060mg
Carbohydrate 34g (Dietary Fiber 4g)
Protein 28g

% DAILY VALUE: Vitamin A 28%; Vitamin C 22%; Calcium 14%; Iron 12%

DIET EXCHANGES: 2 Starch, 2 1/2 Very Lean Meat 1 Vegetable

Chicken & Corn Bread Stuffing Casserole

asian chicken salad with peanut-soy dressing

LOW FAT / LOW CHOLESTEROL / LOW CALORIE

PREP: 15 min
6 SERVINGS

Peanut-Soy Dressing (below)

6 cups coleslaw mix

3 cups washed fresh spinach leaves
(from 10-ounce bag)

3 cups chopped cooked chicken

1 medium bell pepper, thinly sliced

1 can (8 ounces) bamboo shoots, rinsed
and drained

Make Peanut-Soy Dressing. Toss remaining ingredients in large bowl. Drizzle with dressing. Serve immediately.

Peanut-Soy Dressing

3 tablespoons reduced-sodium soy sauce

3 tablespoons cider vinegar

2 tablespoons honey

1 tablespoon creamy peanut butter

1/2 teaspoon crushed red pepper

1/2 teaspoon grated gingerroot

Beat all ingredients with wire whisk until blended.

NUTRITION INFORMATION
1 Serving

Calories 300 (Calories from Fat 90)
Fat 10g (Saturated 3g)
Cholesterol 90mg
Sodium 550mg
Carbohydrate 24g (Dietary Fiber 6g)
Protein 35g

% DAILY VALUE: Vitamin A 46%; Vitamin C
100%; Calcium 10%; Iron 18%

DIET EXCHANGES: 3 1/3 Very Lean Meat,
5 Vegetable

country turkey stroganoff

LOW FAT / LOW CHOLESTEROL

PREP: 10 min **COOK:** 15 min
4 SERVINGS

Savor the rich "stroganoff" flavors that come through in this home-style dish, without all the fat. Try pairing it with steamed broccoli drizzled with a squirt of lemon juice and a basket of hearty brown bread.

1 can (10 ounces) condensed 98% fat-free cream of chicken soup

1/4 cup reduced-fat sour cream

2 tablespoons fat-free (skim) milk

1 tablespoon Worcestershire sauce

1/4 teaspoon salt

3 cups uncooked cholesterol-free noodles (6 ounces)

3/4 pound turkey breast tenderloins or boneless, skinless chicken breast halves

2 medium onions, chopped (1 cup)

1 package (8 ounces) sliced mushrooms (3 cups)

2 tablespoons chopped fresh parsley

Beat soup, sour cream, milk, Worcestershire sauce and salt with wire whisk until blended; set aside. Cook and drain noodles as directed on package.

Remove fat from turkey. Cut turkey into 1-inch pieces. Spray 10-inch nonstick skillet with cooking spray; heat over medium-high heat. Cook turkey in skillet about 5 minutes, stirring frequently, until no longer pink in center. Remove turkey from skillet; keep warm.

Spray skillet with cooking spray. Cook onions in skillet over medium-high heat 3 minutes, stirring constantly. Stir in mushrooms. Cook 4 minutes, stirring frequently; reduce heat to low. Stir in soup mixture and turkey. Cook 2 to 3 minutes, stirring frequently, until heated through (do not boil). Serve turkey mixture over noodles. Sprinkle with parsley.

NUTRITION INFORMATION
1 Serving

Calories 355 (Calories from Fat 45)
Fat 5g (Saturated 2g)
Cholesterol 65mg
Sodium 690mg
Carbohydrate 49g (Dietary Fiber 3g)
Protein 31g

% DAILY VALUE: Vitamin A 6%; Vitamin C 6%; Calcium 6%; Iron 22%

DIET EXCHANGES: 3 Starch, 3 Very Lean Meat, 1 Vegetable

turkey tenderloins with cranberry stuffing

LOW FAT / LOW CHOLESTEROL / LOW CALORIE

PREP: 15 min **BAKE:** 45 min
4 SERVINGS

A sweet-tart cranberry stuffing tucked into tender turkey pockets lets you savor the flavors of Thanksgiving without the holiday guilt. Top off the meal with a slimmed-down slice of Streusel Pumpkin Pie (page 197).

1 pound turkey breast tenderloins

1/2 cup dried cranberries

2 tablespoons firmly packed brown sugar

1 1/2 cups soft bread cubes (about 3 slices bread)

1/2 teaspoon grated orange peel

2 tablespoons orange juice

1/4 teaspoon salt

1/4 teaspoon ground nutmeg

2 medium green onions, sliced (2 tablespoons)

Nutmeg-Orange Sauce (right)

Heat oven to 400°. Spray square pan, 9 × 9 × 2 inches, with cooking spray. Cut pocket lengthwise in each turkey breast tenderloin to within 1/2 inch of ends.

Mix cranberries and brown sugar in medium bowl. Stir in remaining ingredients except Nutmeg-Orange Sauce. Spoon into pockets in turkey; secure with toothpicks. Place in pan.

Cover and bake 40 to 45 minutes or until juice of turkey is no longer pink when centers of thickest pieces are cut.

Make Nutmeg-Orange Sauce. Cut turkey into slices. Serve sauce with turkey.

Nutmeg-Orange Sauce

1 tablespoon cornstarch

1/8 teaspoon ground nutmeg

Dash of salt

1 cup orange juice

Mix cornstarch, nutmeg and salt in 1 1/2-quart saucepan. Gradually stir in orange juice. Cook over medium heat, stirring constantly, until mixture thickens and boils. Boil and stir 1 minute.

NUTRITION INFORMATION
1 Serving

Calories 275 (Calories from Fat 20)
Fat 3g (Saturated 1g)
Cholesterol 75mg
Sodium 160mg
Carbohydrate 41g (Dietary Fiber 6g)
Protein 29g

% DAILY VALUE: Vitamin A 2%; Vitamin C 34%; Calcium 4%; Iron 14%

DIET EXCHANGES: 1 Starch, 3 Very Lean Meat, 1 1/2 Fruit

Turkey Tenderloins with Cranberry Stuffing

grilled sesame-ginger turkey slices

LOW FAT / LOW CHOLESTEROL / LOW CALORIE

PREP: 5 min **GRILL:** 10 min
4 SERVINGS

Turkey breast slices may be tricky to find. If they're not available in your supermarket, use boneless, skinless turkey breast tenderloins, pounded to 1/4-inch thickness.

2 tablespoons teriyaki sauce

1 tablespoon sesame seed, toasted*

1 teaspoon ground ginger

1 pound uncooked turkey breast slices, about 1/4 inch thick

Hot cooked noodles or rice, if desired

2 medium green onions, sliced (2 tablespoons)

Heat coals or gas grill. Mix teriyaki sauce, sesame seed and ginger.

Cover and grill turkey 4 to 6 inches from medium heat 8 to 10 minutes, turning and brushing with sauce mixture after 5 minutes, until turkey is no longer pink in center. Discard any remaining sauce mixture. Serve turkey with noodles. Sprinkle with onions.

To toast sesame seed, bake uncovered in ungreased shallow pan in 350° oven 8 to 10 minutes, stirring occasionally, until golden brown. Or cook in ungreased heavy skillet over medium heat about 2 minutes, stirring frequently until browning begins, then stirring constantly until golden brown.

NUTRITION INFORMATION
1 Serving

Calories 135 (Calories from Fat 20)
Fat 2g (Saturated 0g)
Cholesterol 75mg
Sodium 390mg
Carbohydrate 2g (Dietary Fiber 0g)
Protein 27g

% DAILY VALUE: Vitamin A 0%; Vitamin C 0%; Calcium 2%; Iron 8%

DIET EXCHANGES: 4 Very Lean Meat

Grilled Sesame-Ginger Turkey Slices

Sometimes eating out is a treat; sometimes it's a necessity. Regardless of whether it is fine dining or dinner in a dash, the tips for trimming the fat are the same.

1. Choose the restaurant wisely.

   Consider your health goals as you plan where you want to eat. Some restaurants are more willing to accommodate special requests than others. To avoid overeating, curb your appetite with a piece of fruit or a large glass of water before you go.

2. Develop a game plan.

   Have in mind what you plan to order before arriving at the restaurant. You may even decide not to open up the menu so that the double-decker burger and fries or the oil-drenched plate of pasta does not tempt you. If you do take a peek at the menu, look only at what you really want to eat, like the fresh salads, not the heavy dinner entrées or rich desserts.

3. Ask for what you want.

   Find out how foods are prepared, then ask for adjustments. Request sauces and dressings on the side, less oil or butter in preparation, etc. Substitute fat-free salad dressing or salsa for sour cream and butter on your baked potato.

4. Size up the portion sizes.

   Many restaurants serve very large portions. Ask for a half-portion or lunch-size meal, or split an entrée with your companion. Check out low-fat appetizer options as a possible meal. Get comfortable with leaving food on your plate. Ask for the server's help in having your plate taken away from the table or put a napkin over your food when feeling full so you won't continue to be tempted.

5. Become fluent in menu-ese.

   Choose menu items that are baked, grilled, blackened, broiled, roasted or steamed. Let your server know that you're on a healthy track.

6. Watch the pre-meal warm-up.

   Move the complimentary basket of chips and dip away from where you're sitting. Instead of spreading butter on your bread or dipping it in olive oil, enjoy it plain. Use a light hand at the salad bar; pick primarily fresh veggies versus the higher-fat accessory items such as marinated or mayonnaise-based salads, cheeses, bacon flavor bits, chopped eggs and olives.

7. Decide on dessert.

   Fresh fruit is always a good bet when you want a sweet finish to your meal. If the fruit is dressed in a decadent sauce, ask for the topping on the side so you can drizzle on a delicious taste. Sorbet and frozen yogurt are other low-fat dessert winners. If you're craving something rich and creamy, how about a cappuccino or latte made with fat-free (skim) milk and a sprinkle of chocolate?

8. Take it home.

   Leftovers are a good thing. Start out by asking your server to box up half of whatever you're about to order. Or when your plate arrives, split it in half before you dig in.

caesar turkey subs

LOW FAT / LOW CHOLESTEROL / LOW CALORIE

PREP: 15 min
4 SERVINGS

4 sub rolls or one 8-ounce baguette

2 tablespoons balsamic or red wine vinegar

24 slices turkey pepperoni

4 slices tomato, cut in half

2 cups shredded lettuce

1/2 medium red onion, thinly sliced

1/2 medium bell pepper, cut into thin strips

1/4 cup fat-free Caesar dressing

1/2 cup shredded low-fat mozzarella cheese (2 ounces)

Cut rolls horizontally in half (if using baguette, first cut into fourths). Drizzle vinegar over bottom halves. Top with pepperoni, tomato, lettuce, onion and bell pepper. Drizzle with dressing. Sprinkle with cheese. Top with roll tops; press gently. Cut each sandwich diagonally in half.

NUTRITION INFORMATION
1 Serving

Calories 300 (Calories from Fat 80)
Fat 9g (Saturated 4g)
Cholesterol 40mg
Sodium 1270mg
Carbohydrate 39g (Dietary Fiber 3g)
Protein 19g

% DAILY VALUE: Vitamin A 12%; Vitamin C 26%; Calcium 16%; Iron 14%

DIET EXCHANGES: 2 Starch, 2 Lean Meat, 2 Vegetable

cornmeal-crusted catfish

LOW FAT / LOW CHOLESTEROL / LOW CALORIE

PREP: 10 min **BAKE:** 15 min
4 SERVINGS

1/4 cup yellow cornmeal

1/4 cup dry bread crumbs

1 teaspoon chili powder

1/2 teaspoon paprika

1/2 teaspoon garlic salt

1/4 teaspoon pepper

1 pound catfish fillets, about 3/4 inch thick

1/4 cup fat-free ranch dressing

Chopped fresh parsley, if desired

Heat oven to 450°. Spray broiler-pan rack with cooking spray. Mix cornmeal, bread crumbs, chili powder, paprika, garlic salt and pepper.

Remove and discard skin from fish. Cut fish into 4 serving pieces. Lightly brush dressing on all sides of fish. Coat fish with cornmeal mixture. Place fish on rack in broiler pan. Bake uncovered about 15 minutes or until fish flakes easily with fork. Sprinkle with parsley.

NUTRITION INFORMATION
1 Serving

Calories 170 (Calories from Fat 20)
Fat 2g (Saturated 0g)
Cholesterol 60mg
Sodium 300mg
Carbohydrate 16g (Dietary Fiber 1g)
Protein 23g

% DAILY VALUE: Vitamin A 4%; Vitamin C 0%; Calcium 6%; Iron 6%

DIET EXCHANGES: 1 Starch, 2 1/2 Very Lean Meat

Cornmeal-Crusted Catfish

parmesan-basil perch

LOW FAT / LOW CHOLESTEROL / LOW CALORIE

PREP: 10 min **BAKE:** 20 min
4 SERVINGS

1 pound ocean perch, red snapper, or orange roughy fillets, about 1/2 inch thick

2 tablespoons dry bread crumbs

1 tablespoon grated reduced-fat or fat-free Parmesan cheese topping

1 tablespoon chopped fresh or 1 teaspoon dried basil leaves

1/2 teaspoon paprika

Dash of pepper

1 tablespoon margarine, melted

2 tablespoons chopped fresh parsley

Move oven rack to position slightly above middle of oven. Heat oven to 375°. Spray rectangular pan, 13 × 9 × 2 inches, with cooking spray. Cut fish into 4 serving pieces.

Mix remaining ingredients except margarine and parsley. Brush one side of fish pieces with margarine; dip into crumb mixture. Place fish, coated sides up, in pan.

Bake uncovered 15 to 20 minutes or until fish flakes easily with fork. Sprinkle with parsley.

NUTRITION INFORMATION
1 Serving

Calories 135 (Calories from Fat 45)
Fat 5g (Saturated 1g)
Cholesterol 55mg
Sodium 170mg
Carbohydrate 3g (Dietary Fiber 0g)
Protein 20g

% DAILY VALUE: Vitamin A 6%; Vitamin C 2%; Calcium 4%; Iron 2%

DIET EXCHANGES: 3 Very Lean Meat, 1/2 Fat

HEALTHY CONVENIENCE

Time is not on most people's side these days. It's a grab-and-go way of life. Can healthy foods fit in? Not a problem; here's how:

At the grocery store

- Pick up the precut, prewashed, ready-to-eat produce. It may cost more, but "time is money."
- Buy sliced deli meats, such as turkey and lean ham or roast beef. Select whole-grain buns or bread to make sandwiches.
- Try the deli's fresh vegetable salads that are mixed with vinegar, not mayonnaise.
- Look for carryout items or quick meal solutions that use lean meats or fish.
- Select frozen or boxed dinner mixes, leaving out meat as an ingredient and tossing in extra veggies.
- Pick whole-grain side dishes, such as brown rice or whole wheat pasta.

At the fast-food restaurant

- Bigger is not better; stick with regular-size portions.
- Hold the add-ons, such as sauces and cheese. Get clever with toppings. If you choose a baked potato, fill it with salsa, not sour cream, or tap into the salad bar's veggies for a different twist.
- Steer clear of fried foods and breaded or multilayered sandwiches—simplicity usually saves fat.

Thinking of takeout?

- If you choose Chinese, bypass the "batter-coated" and "crispy" (a.k.a. deep-fried) items on the menu, and stick with stir-fried vegetables and a side of steamed rice.
- Picking up a pizza? Opt for the thin-crust variety, pile on the veggies and go light on the cheese.
- Conquering the mealtime madness with Mexican? Pass up the overstuffed burrito with beef and refried beans, and forget the fat-laden toppings such as cheese, sour cream and guacamole. Tempt your taste buds instead with a grilled chicken, bean or vegetable burrito with an extra side of salsa.

On the road or in the air

- Stash portable fruit, such as an apple or orange, in your car or briefcase.
- Put nonperishable foods, such as whole-grain cereal or crackers, dried fruits or low-fat cookies such as fig bars and vanilla wafers, in your glove compartment.
- When traveling by plane, request a low-fat or vegetarian meal, or carry your own healthy snacks. Drink plenty of water to stay fresh, energetic and headache free. As a general rule, drink one cup of water for every hour in the air.

grilled creole snapper

LOW FAT / LOW CHOLESTEROL / LOW CALORIE

PREP: 15 min **GRILL:** 14 min
4 SERVINGS

The chunky topping of grilled veggies that crowns these southern-spiced fillets makes this a perfect summertime dish. For a crisp and cooling sidekick, toss together a salad of leafy greens and sliced fresh tomatoes.

2 medium tomatoes, cut crosswise in half

1 medium onion, cut into fourths

1/2 medium green bell pepper, cut in half

4 medium green onions, thinly sliced (1/4 cup)

1 1/2 tablespoons red wine vinegar

1/2 teaspoon dried thyme leaves

1/2 teaspoon salt

1/4 teaspoon red pepper sauce

1 1/2 pounds red snapper, sole or flounder fillets, about 1/2 inch thick

Cooking spray

2 tablespoons chopped fresh parsley

Hot cooked rice, if desired

Heat coals or gas grill. Spray large piece of heavy-duty aluminum foil with cooking spray. Place tomatoes, onion and bell pepper on foil. Wrap foil securely around vegetables. Cover and grill foil packets, seam sides up, 4 to 6 inches from medium heat 6 minutes, turning once.

While vegetables are grilling, mix green onions, vinegar, thyme, salt and pepper sauce; set aside.

Spray fish and hinged wire grill basket with cooking spray. Place fish in basket. Cover and grill fish 7 to 8 minutes, turning once, until fish flakes easily with fork.

Place fish on serving platter; keep warm. Coarsely chop grilled vegetables. Toss vegetables, parsley, and green onion mixture; spoon over fish. Serve with rice.

NUTRITION INFORMATION
1 Serving

Calories 160 (Calories from Fat 20)
Fat 2g (Saturated 0g)
Cholesterol 80mg
Sodium 130mg
Carbohydrate 8g (Dietary Fiber 2g)
Protein 29g

% DAILY VALUE: Vitamin A 8%; Vitamin C 2%; Calcium 4%; Iron 6%

DIET EXCHANGES: 4 Very Lean Meat, 1 Vegetable

Grilled Creole Snapper

broiled caribbean swordfish

LOW FAT / LOW CHOLESTEROL / LOW CALORIE

PREP: 10 min **MARINATE:** 2 hr **BROIL:** 16 min
4 SERVINGS

Who doesn't long for a taste of the Tropics? This dish will take you there without your ever leaving the kitchen. If tropical fruits tickle your taste buds, try fresh pineapple, mango or guava tossed in with the papaya, and get an extra boost of vitamin C.

4 swordfish or shark steaks, 1 inch thick
(about 1 1/2 pounds)

1 tablespoon grated lime peel

1/4 cup lime juice

1/4 cup grapefruit juice

1/2 teaspoon salt

1 clove garlic, finely chopped

Papaya Salsa (below)

Place fish in ungreased square baking dish, 8 × 8 × 2 inches. Mix lime peel, lime juice, grapefruit juice, salt and garlic; pour over fish. Cover and refrigerate 2 hours. Make Papaya Salsa.

Set oven control to broil. Spray broiler-pan rack with cooking spray. Remove fish from marinade; reserve marinade. Place fish on rack in broiler pan. Broil with tops about 4 inches from heat about 16 minutes, turning and brushing with marinade after 8 minutes, until fish flakes easily with fork. Discard any remaining marinade. Serve fish with salsa.

Papaya Salsa

1 large papaya, peeled, seeded, and chopped (2 cups)

1 medium green onion, finely chopped (1 tablespoon)

1/4 cup finely chopped red bell pepper

1 tablespoon chopped fresh cilantro

2 to 3 tablespoons grapefruit juice

1/8 teaspoon salt

Mix all ingredients in glass or plastic bowl. Cover and refrigerate 1 hour.

NUTRITION INFORMATION
1 Serving

Calories 220 (Calories from Fat 65)
Fat 7g (Saturated 2g)
Cholesterol 80mg
Sodium 80mg
Carbohydrate 14g (Dietary Fiber 2g)
Protein 27g

% DAILY VALUE: Vitamin A 12%; Vitamin C 74%; Calcium 4%; Iron 6%

DIET EXCHANGES: 4 Very Lean Meat, 1 Fruit, 1/2 Fat

salmon teriyaki

LOW FAT / LOW CHOLESTEROL / LOW CALORIE

PREP: 10 min **MARINATE:** 1 hr **BROIL:** 6 min
4 SERVINGS

1 pound salmon fillets, about 3/4 inch thick

1/4 cup soy sauce

1/3 cup dry white wine or orange juice

1/2 cup packed brown sugar

1 teaspoon ground ginger

Remove and discard skin from fish. Cut fish into 4 serving pieces. Mix soy sauce, wine, brown sugar and ginger in shallow glass or plastic dish. Add fish; turn several times to coat. Cover and refrigerate 1 hour, turning once.

Set oven control to broil. Spray broiler-pan rack with cooking spray. Remove fish from marinade; reserve marinade. Place fish on rack in broiler pan. Brush with marinade. Broil with tops about 4 inches from heat 5 to 6 minutes or until fish flakes easily with fork. Discard any remaining marinade.

NUTRITION INFORMATION
1 Serving

Calories 215 (Calories from Fat 55)
Fat 6g (Saturated 2g)
Cholesterol 65mg
Sodium 980mg
Carbohydrate 19g (Dietary Fiber 0g)
Protein 21g

% DAILY VALUE: Vitamin A 2%; Vitamin C 0%; Calcium 2%; Iron 8%

DIET EXCHANGES: 1 Starch, 3 Very Lean Meat, 1/2 Fruit

scallops with red pepper sauce

LOW FAT / LOW CHOLESTEROL / LOW CALORIE

PREP: 20 min **COOK:** 5 min
4 SERVINGS

Red pepper sauce is a fiery little number made with peppers, vinegar and salt. Many brands are available, and the heat varies greatly among them. Some are so hot that just a drop is enough; others are milder, allowing you to be more generous, so pick your favorite!

1 large red bell pepper, cut into fourths

1/8 teaspoon salt

10 drops red pepper sauce

1 clove garlic, finely chopped

1/4 cup plain fat-free yogurt

1 pound bay scallops

4 medium green onions, sliced (1/4 cup)

Fresh cilantro leaves

Hot cooked pasta or rice, if desired

Place steamer basket in 1/2 inch water in saucepan or skillet (water should not touch bottom of basket). Place bell pepper in basket. Cover tightly and heat to boiling; reduce heat to medium-low. Steam 8 to 10 minutes or until tender.

Place bell pepper, salt, pepper sauce and garlic in blender or food processor. Cover and blend on medium speed until almost smooth. Heat bell pepper mixture in 1-quart saucepan over medium heat, stirring occasionally, until hot; remove from heat. Gradually stir in yogurt; keep warm.

Spray 10-inch nonstick skillet with cooking spray; heat over medium-high heat. Add scallops and onions; stir-fry 4 to 5 minutes or until scallops are white. Serve sauce with scallops. Garnish with cilantro. Serve with pasta.

NUTRITION INFORMATION
1 Serving

Calories 90 (Calories from Fat 10)
Fat 1g (Saturated 0g)
Cholesterol 20mg
Sodium 240mg
Carbohydrate 7g (Dietary Fiber 1g)
Protein 14g

% DAILY VALUE: Vitamin A 26%; Vitamin C 66%; Calcium 10%; Iron 12%

DIET EXCHANGES: 2 Very Lean Meat, 1 Vegetable

lemon-dill shrimp

LOW FAT / LOW CALORIE

PREP: 10 min **COOK:** 6 min
4 SERVINGS

Fresh dill weed has no equal in the world of dried herbs. Its feathery green leaves lend a distinctive flavor to any dish. Because fresh dill weed loses its flavor quickly during cooking, adding it at the very end is best.

2 tablespoons lemon juice

1 tablespoon olive or vegetable oil

1 1/2 teaspoons chopped fresh dill weed

1/4 teaspoon salt

1 pound uncooked peeled deveined medium shrimp, thawed if frozen

Hot cooked rice, if desired

Mix lemon juice, oil, dill weed and salt; set aside.

Spray 10-inch nonstick skillet with cooking spray; heat over medium heat. Cook shrimp in skillet over medium heat about 5 minutes, stirring frequently, until pink and firm. Remove shrimp from skillet, using slotted spoon. Drain well on paper towels.

Wipe out skillet with paper towel. Add shrimp and lemon juice mixture to skillet. Cook about 1 minute over medium heat, stirring frequently, until heated through. Serve with rice.

NUTRITION INFORMATION
1 Serving

Calories 85 (Calories from Fat 35)
Fat 4g (Saturated 1g)
Cholesterol 105mg
Sodium 125mg
Carbohydrate 1g (Dietary Fiber 0g)
Protein 11g

% DAILY VALUE: Vitamin A 2%; Vitamin C 4%; Calcium 2%; Iron 10%

DIET EXCHANGES: 1 1/2 Lean Meat

sweet apricot BBQ shrimp kabobs

LOW FAT / LOW CALORIE

PREP: 20 min **BROIL:** 12 min
4 SERVINGS

Shrimp are fairly high in cholesterol, but they're low in saturated fat and total fat. You can enjoy shrimp as part of a low-fat, low-cholesterol diet, just be sure to watch your total cholesterol intake for each day.

1/3 cup hickory-smoked barbecue sauce

1/3 cup apricot preserves

1/4 teaspoon crushed red pepper

4 slices turkey bacon, each cut lengthwise into 6 strips

1 can (8 ounces) whole water chestnuts, drained

1 pound uncooked peeled deveined large shrimp, thawed if frozen

Hot cooked rice, if desired

Set oven control to broil. Mix barbecue sauce, preserves and red pepper; set aside.

Wrap strip of bacon around each water chestnut. Thread shrimp and water chestnuts alternately on each of four 10-inch bamboo skewers,* leaving space between each piece.

Broil kabobs with tops about 4 inches from heat 6 minutes, brushing frequently with sauce mixture. Turn kabobs; brush with sauce mixture. Broil 5 to 6 minutes longer or until shrimp are pink and firm. Discard any remaining sauce mixture. Serve kabobs with rice.

*If using bamboo skewers, soak in water at least 30 minutes before using to prevent burning.

NUTRITION INFORMATION
1 Serving

Calories 185 (Calories from Fat 35)
Fat 4g (Saturated 1g)
Cholesterol 95mg
Sodium 390mg
Carbohydrate 25g (Dietary Fiber 1g)
Protein 13g

% DAILY VALUE: Vitamin A 4%; Vitamin C 6%; Calcium 4%; Iron 10%

DIET EXCHANGES: 2 Lean Meat, 1 1/2 Fruit

Sweet Apricot BBQ Shrimp Kabobs

low fat

Main-dish recipes have 10 or fewer grams of fat per serving.
Low-fat side dishes and desserts have 3 or fewer grams of fat per serving.

low cholesterol

Recipes have 90 or fewer milligrams of cholesterol per serving.

low calorie

Recipes have 350 or fewer calories per serving with the exception of desserts.
Low-calorie desserts have 250 or fewer calories per serving.

CHAPTER 3

beef, pork & lamb

Panfried Ham with Sweet Balsamic-Peach Sauce (page 113)

three-pepper beef tenderloin

LOW FAT / LOW CHOLESTEROL / LOW CALORIE

PREP: 10 min **MARINATE:** 2 hr **ROAST:** 40 min **STAND:** 15 min
6 SERVINGS

This spicy peppered steak is not for timid taste buds! Serve with a baked potato and a crisp green salad to help balance the spiciness.

1 1/2-pound beef tenderloin

1 tablespoon freshly ground black pepper

2 teaspoons white pepper

2 teaspoons fennel seed, crushed

1/2 teaspoon salt

1/2 teaspoon ground thyme

1/4 teaspoon ground red pepper (cayenne)

Remove fat from beef. Mix remaining ingredients; rub over beef. Cover and refrigerate at least 2 hours but no longer than 24 hours.

Heat oven to 350°. Spray shallow roasting pan with cooking spray. Place beef in pan. Insert meat thermometer so tip is in center of thickest part of beef. Roast uncovered about 40 minutes or until thermometer reads 140° (medium-rare doneness). Cover beef loosely with tent of aluminum foil and let stand about 15 minutes. (Temperature will continue to rise about 5°, and beef will be easier to carve as juices set up.) Cut beef across grain at slanted angle into thin slices.

THE LEANEST CUTS OF BEEF

These are lean times for the beef industry. It's not sales that are trim, it's the size of the steers. Cattle are bred today to be "slimmer" than cattle bred nearly thirty years ago. That makes red meat a more healthy choice than in previous years. Take a look at the six leanest cuts of beef.

The Skinniest Six

Cut*	Fat(g)	Saturated Fat(g)
Tenderloin	8	3.0
Top loin	7	1.5
Top sirloin	6	2.5
Round tip	5	2.0
Top round	4	1.5
Eye of round	4	1.5

*Portion size: 3 ounces

NUTRITION INFORMATION
1 Serving

Calories 125 (Calories from Fat 55)
Fat 6g (Saturated 2g)
Cholesterol 50mg
Sodium 240mg
Carbohydrate 1g (Dietary Fiber 0g)
Protein 18g

% DAILY VALUE: Vitamin A 0%; Vitamin C 0%; Calcium 2%; Iron 10%

DIET EXCHANGES: 2 1/2 Lean Meat

beef with spiced pepper sauce

LOW FAT / LOW CHOLESTEROL / LOW CALORIE

PREP: 10 min **COOK:** 17 min
4 SERVINGS

If you're watching your salt intake, try reduced-sodium soy sauce. It has 50 percent less sodium than regular soy sauce, but it still has the same great flavor!

1-pound beef top sirloin steak, about 3/4 inch thick

3 tablespoons ketchup

3 tablespoons water

3/4 teaspoon soy sauce

1/2 medium green bell pepper, cut into thin strips

1 small onion, thinly sliced

Coarsely ground pepper

Remove fat from beef. Place beef between 2 sheets of plastic wrap or waxed paper. Pound beef with meat mallet or rolling pin to tenderize. Cut beef into 4 serving pieces.

Beat ketchup, water and soy sauce with wire whisk until blended; set aside.

Spray 10-inch nonstick skillet with cooking spray; heat over medium-high heat. Cook beef in skillet 3 minutes, turning once. Add bell pepper and onion. Stir in ketchup mixture; reduce heat to low. Cover and simmer 12 minutes. Remove beef from skillet; keep warm.

Stir ground pepper into sauce in skillet; heat to boiling. Boil 2 minutes, stirring frequently, until sauce is slightly thickened. Serve sauce over beef.

NUTRITION INFORMATION
1 Serving

Calories 130 (Calories from Fat 25)
Fat 3g (Saturated 1g)
Cholesterol 50mg
Sodium 180mg
Carbohydrate 6g (Dietary Fiber 0g)
Protein 20g

% DAILY VALUE: Vitamin A 2%; Vitamin C 12%; Calcium 0%; Iron 10%

DIET EXCHANGES: 3 Very Lean Meat, 1 Vegetable

chilied beef wrap

LOW FAT / LOW CHOLESTEROL / LOW CALORIE

PREP: 20 min **BROIL:** 10 min
4 SERVINGS

1-pound beef top sirloin steak, about 3/4 inch thick

1 1/2 tablespoons chili powder

2 teaspoons dried oregano leaves

1 teaspoon ground cumin

1 teaspoon salt

4 fat-free flour tortillas (6 to 8 inches in diameter)

3/4 cup fat-free sour cream

1 tablespoon prepared horseradish

4 cups shredded lettuce

1 large tomato, chopped (1 cup)

Remove fat from beef. Mix chili powder, oregano, cumin and 1/2 teaspoon salt. Rub mixture on both sides of beef. Let stand 10 minutes at room temperature.

Set oven control to broil. Place beef on rack in broiler pan. Broil with top 3 to 4 inches from heat about 5 minutes on each side for medium doneness or until beef is desired doneness. Cut into 1/8-inch slices.

Warm tortillas as directed on package. Mix sour cream, horseradish and remaining 1/2 teaspoon salt. Spread 3 tablespoons horseradish mixture over each tortilla; top each with 1 cup of the lettuce and 1/4 cup of the tomato. Top with beef. Fold one end of tortilla up about 1 inch over filling; fold right and left sides over folded end, overlapping. Fold remaining end down.

NUTRITION INFORMATION
1 Serving

Calories 240 (Calories from Fat 55)
Fat 6g (Saturated 2g)
Cholesterol 55mg
Sodium 830mg
Carbohydrate 23g (Dietary Fiber 3g)
Protein 26g

% DAILY VALUE: Vitamin A 22%; Vitamin C 24%; Calcium 16%; Iron 22%

DIET EXCHANGES: 1 Starch, 3 Very Lean Meat, 2 Vegetable

Chilied Beef Wrap

hearty beef & vegetables

LOW FAT / LOW CHOLESTEROL / LOW CALORIE

PREP: 10 min **COOK:** 18 min
4 SERVINGS

Don't be tempted to simmer this stew for too long. Although the carrots may not appear to be quite tender when you take the pot off the stove, allowing the mixture to stand for a few minutes will help cook the carrots without turning the potatoes into mush.

1 pound beef top sirloin steak, about 3/4 inch thick

1 bag (16 ounces) frozen stew vegetables, thawed and drained

1 cup frozen cut green beans, thawed and drained

1/2 cup water

1 tablespoon Worcestershire sauce

1/2 package (2-ounce size) onion soup mix (1 envelope)

3 tablespoons chopped fresh parsley

Remove fat from beef. Cut beef into 1/2-inch pieces. Spray 4-quart Dutch oven with cooking spray; heat over medium-high heat. Cook beef in Dutch oven 2 minutes, stirring constantly.

Stir in stew vegetables, green beans, water, Worcestershire sauce and soup mix (dry). Heat to boiling; reduce heat to low. Cover and simmer 12 to 14 minutes, stirring occasionally, until potatoes are just tender; remove from heat. Stir in parsley.

NUTRITION INFORMATION
1 Serving

Calories 95 (Calories from Fat 20)
Fat 2g (Saturated 1g)
Cholesterol 35mg
Sodium 460mg
Carbohydrate 6g (Dietary Fiber 3g)
Protein 16g

% DAILY VALUE: Vitamin A 26%; Vitamin C 22%; Calcium 4%; Iron 10%

DIET EXCHANGES: 2 Very Lean Meat, 1 Vegetable

steakhouse sirloin au jus

LOW FAT / LOW CHOLESTEROL / LOW CALORIE

PREP: 10 min **COOK:** 15 min

4 SERVINGS

1 1/4 cups fat-free beef broth

1 tablespoon Worcestershire sauce

1 tablespoon balsamic or red wine vinegar

1/2 teaspoon sugar

2 cloves garlic, finely chopped

1-pound beef boneless sirloin steak, about 3/4 inch thick

1/4 cup chopped fresh parsley

Freshly ground pepper

Beat broth, Worcestershire sauce, vinegar, sugar and garlic with wire whisk until blended; set aside.

Spray 10-inch nonstick skillet with cooking spray; heat over medium-high heat. Cook beef in skillet 8 to 10 minutes, turning once, until brown. Remove beef from skillet; keep warm.

Add broth mixture to skillet; heat to boiling. Boil 5 minutes, stirring constantly, until sauce is reduced to 1/3 cup; remove from heat.

Cut beef across grain at slanted angle into thin slices. Serve sauce over beef. Sprinkle with parsley and pepper.

NUTRITION INFORMATION
1 Serving

Calories 115 (Calories from Fat 25)
Fat 3g (Saturated 1g)
Cholesterol 50mg
Sodium 400mg
Carbohydrate 2g (Dietary Fiber 0g)
Protein 21g

% DAILY VALUE: Vitamin A 2%; Vitamin C 4%; Calcium 2%; Iron 12%

DIET EXCHANGES: 3 Very Lean Meat

glazed beef tenderloin with herbed new potatoes

PREP: 15 min **MARINATE:** 1 hr **GRILL:** 13 min
4 SERVINGS

1/3 cup steak sauce

1 1/2 tablespoons packed brown sugar

4 beef tenderloin steaks, about 1 inch thick (1 pound)

8 small new potatoes (1 pound), cut lengthwise in half

2 tablespoons water

Cooking spray

1 teaspoon chopped fresh or 1/4 teaspoon dried rosemary leaves, crumbled

1 teaspoon chopped fresh or 1/4 teaspoon dried thyme leaves

1/4 teaspoon paprika

1/2 teaspoon salt

1/4 teaspoon pepper

Mix steak sauce and brown sugar in shallow glass or plastic dish; reserve 2 tablespoons sauce. Add beef to remaining sauce (about 1/4 cup); turn to coat with sauce. Cover and refrigerate, turning beef 2 or 3 times, at least 1 hour but no longer than 24 hours.

Spray grill rack with cooking spray. Heat coals or gas grill for direct heat.

Place potatoes and water in 2-quart microwavable casserole. Cover and microwave on High 3 to 5 minutes or until potatoes are just tender. Place potatoes on sheet of heavy-duty aluminum foil. Spray potatoes with cooking spray; sprinkle with rosemary, thyme and paprika. Wrap securely in foil.

Grill beef and potatoes uncovered 4 to 6 inches from medium heat 7 minutes. Turn beef and potatoes; brush reserved sauce over beef. Grill about 6 minutes longer for medium beef doneness; remove from heat. Sprinkle salt and pepper over potatoes.

To Broil: Marinate beef and microwave potatoes as directed. Spray potatoes with cooking spray; sprinkle with rosemary, thyme and paprika, but do not wrap in foil. Set oven control to broil. Place beef and potatoes on rack in broiler pan. Broil with tops 4 to 6 inches from heat 8 minutes. Turn beef and potatoes; brush reserved sauce over beef. Broil about 7 minutes longer for medium beef doneness.

NUTRITION INFORMATION
1 Serving

Calories 260 (Calories from Fat 65)
Fat 7g (Saturated 3g)
Cholesterol 55mg
Sodium 660mg
Carbohydrate 28g (Dietary Fiber 2g)
Protein 23g

% DAILY VALUE: Vitamin A 2%; Vitamin C 10%; Calcium 2%; Iron 18%

DIET EXCHANGES: 2 Starch, 2 Lean Meat

Glazed Beef Tenderloin with Herbed New Potatoes

swiss steak

LOW FAT / LOW CHOLESTEROL / LOW CALORIE

PREP: 10 min **COOK:** 1 3/4 hr
6 SERVINGS

1 1/2-pound beef boneless round, tip or chuck steak, about 3/4 inch thick

3 tablespoons all-purpose flour

1 teaspoon ground mustard

1/2 teaspoon salt

2 teaspoons vegetable oil

1 can (14 1/2 ounces) whole tomatoes, undrained

2 cloves garlic, finely chopped

1 cup water

1 large onion, sliced

1 large green bell pepper, sliced

Remove fat from beef. Mix flour, mustard and salt. Sprinkle half of the flour mixture over one side of beef; pound in. Turn beef; pound in remaining flour mixture. Cut beef into 6 serving pieces.

Heat oil in 10-inch nonstick skillet over medium heat. Cook beef in oil about 15 minutes, turning once, until brown. Stir in tomatoes and garlic, breaking up tomatoes. Heat to boiling; reduce heat to low. Cover and simmer about 1 1/4 hours or until beef is tender.

Stir in water, onion and bell pepper. Heat to boiling; reduce heat to low. Cover and simmer 5 to 8 minutes or until vegetables are tender.

NUTRITION INFORMATION
1 Serving

Calories 175 (Calories from Fat 45)
Fat 5g (Saturated 1g)
Cholesterol 55mg
Sodium 150mg
Carbohydrate 10g (Dietary Fiber 2g)
Protein 24g

% DAILY VALUE: Vitamin A 6%; Vitamin C 30%; Calcium 4%; Iron 14%

DIET EXCHANGES: 3 Very Lean Meat, 2 Vegetable

GARLIC AND ONIONS FOR GOOD HEALTH

The medicinal properties of garlic and onions have been known in other parts of the world for thousands of years. Now they're grabbing the attention of researchers here. Garlic and onions have been used to help heal wounds, treat tumors and ward off infection. Today, they are being studied for their possible protective role against cancer and heart disease.

Garlic and onions contain sulfur compounds, which some studies suggest may help lower blood cholesterol levels, including LDL cholesterol. Research has suggested that eating half a clove of garlic each day may lower cholesterol by 9 percent. Garlic may also play a role in lowering blood pressure and reducing the tendency for blood to form clots, which could help reduce the risk for a heart attack or stroke.

Using supplements instead of eating garlic and onions has had mixed results. The effectiveness of active ingredients in supplements can vary significantly, plus it is possible to "overdose" on garlic, causing allergic reactions or anemia.

lazy joes

LOW FAT / LOW CHOLESTEROL / LOW CALORIE

PREP: 10 min **COOK:** 20 min
6 SERVINGS

This slim and healthful cousin to sloppy joes would also be great served on multigrain or whole wheat buns for a fiber-rich alternative to the kaiser rolls.

1/2 pound diet-lean or extra-lean ground beef

1 medium onion, chopped (1/2 cup)

1 small green bell pepper, chopped (1/2 cup)

1/2 cup frozen whole kernel corn, thawed

1/3 cup ketchup

1 teaspoon beef bouillon granules

2 teaspoons Worcestershire sauce

1 can (14 1/2 ounces) diced tomatoes, undrained

6 onion kaiser rolls, split and warmed

Spray 10-inch nonstick skillet with cooking spray; heat over medium-high heat. Cook beef, onion and bell pepper in skillet about 5 minutes, stirring frequently, until beef is brown.

Stir in remaining ingredients except rolls. Heat to boiling; reduce heat to low. Simmer uncovered 15 minutes, stirring occasionally. Fill rolls with beef mixture.

NUTRITION INFORMATION
1 Serving

Calories 235 (Calories from Fat 65)
Fat 7g (Saturated 2g)
Cholesterol 20mg
Sodium 750mg
Carbohydrate 33g (Dietary Fiber 3g)
Protein 13g

% DAILY VALUE: Vitamin A 6%; Vitamin C 40%; Calcium 8%; Iron 16%

DIET EXCHANGES: 2 Starch, 1 Lean Meat, 1 Vegetable

LOW-FAT COOKING 101: DRAINING GROUND BEEF

You're likely to find a choice of ground beef in the supermarket, from regular to diet to extra-lean. Even if you choose the leanest cut available (weighing in at about 8 percent fat), you can still shed some extra fat with these quick tips:

Cook ground beef in a nonstick skillet coated with cooking spray. After cooking, spoon cooked beef into a colander to drain off the fat.

If you want to get rid of even more fat, after draining cooked beef, press it between several layers of paper towels. Wipe out the skillet with a paper towel if you are adding other ingredients back to the skillet.

taco-corn chili

LOW FAT / LOW CHOLESTEROL / LOW CALORIE

PREP: 5 min **COOK:** 25 min
4 SERVINGS

Top off this "meal-in-a-bowl" with shredded reduced-fat or fat-free Cheddar cheese and crushed baked tortilla chips. If you like, substitute ground turkey breast or lean ground pork for the ground beef.

1/2 pound diet-lean or extra-lean ground beef

1 can (15 to 16 ounces) reduced-sodium kidney beans, rinsed and drained

1 envelope (1 1/4 ounces) taco seasoning mix

1 can (10 ounces) diced tomatoes and green chilies, undrained

1 package (10 ounces) frozen whole kernel corn, thawed and drained

2 cups water

2 teaspoons sugar

Spray 4-quart Dutch oven with cooking spray; heat over medium-high heat. Cook beef in Dutch oven, stirring occasionally, until brown; drain.

Stir in remaining ingredients. Heat to boiling; reduce heat to low. Simmer uncovered 18 minutes, stirring occasionally.

NUTRITION INFORMATION
1 Serving

Calories 235 (Calories from Fat 55)
Fat 6g (Saturated 2g)
Cholesterol 25mg
Sodium 400mg
Carbohydrate 34g (Dietary Fiber 7g)
Protein 18g

% DAILY VALUE: Vitamin A 10%; Vitamin C 12%; Calcium 6%; Iron 22%

DIET EXCHANGES: 2 Starch, 1 1/2 Very Lean Meat, 1 Vegetable

campfire mesquite beef & beans

LOW FAT / LOW CHOLESTEROL

PREP: 10 min **COOK:** 25 min
4 SERVINGS

For dinner on the run, skip the pasta and wrap up this smoky-tasting stove-top dish in fat-free flour tortillas. For an extra treat, sneak in some fat-free sour cream and a spoonful of salsa.

1/2 pound diet-lean or extra-lean ground beef

2 cups water

1/4 cup mesquite-flavored barbecue sauce

1 tablespoon chili powder

2 teaspoons beef bouillon granules

1 1/2 teaspoons ground cumin

1/2 teaspoon onion powder

1 can (15 to 16 ounces) kidney beans, rinsed and drained

2 cups uncooked wagon wheel pasta (4 ounces)

Spray 4-quart Dutch oven with cooking spray; heat over medium-high heat. Cook beef in Dutch oven, stirring occasionally, until brown; drain.

Stir in remaining ingredients except pasta. Heat to boiling; reduce heat to low. Simmer uncovered 18 minutes, stirring occasionally.

Cook and drain pasta as directed on package. Spoon beef mixture over pasta.

NUTRITION INFORMATION
1 Serving

Calories 355 (Calories from Fat 65)
Fat 7g (Saturated 2g)
Cholesterol 25mg
Sodium 840mg
Carbohydrate 57g (Dietary Fiber 7g)
Protein 23g

% DAILY VALUE: Vitamin A 0%; Vitamin C 2%; Calcium 4%; Iron 30%

DIET EXCHANGES: 3 Starch, 2 Very Lean Meat, 2 Vegetable

Campfire Mesquite Beef & Beans

cajun mustard pork chops

LOW FAT / LOW CHOLESTEROL / LOW CALORIE

PREP: 5 min **COOK:** 12 min

4 SERVINGS

Cajun seasoning blends vary depending on the brand you choose, but most have a bold flavor and a sassy bite. What's in Cajun seasoning? Usually it is a blend of garlic, onions, chilies, black pepper, mustard and celery.

4 pork loin chops, 1/2 inch thick (about 1 1/4 pounds)

4 cloves garlic, cut in half

2 teaspoons Dijon mustard

1/2 teaspoon Cajun seasoning

1/4 teaspoon paprika

Set oven control to broil. Spray broiler pan and its rack with cooking spray. Remove fat from pork. Rub both sides of pork with garlic; discard garlic. Place pork on rack in broiler pan. Mix remaining ingredients; spread 1 teaspoon of the mustard mixture evenly over pork.

Broil pork with tops about 3 inches from heat about 6 minutes. Turn pork; brush with remaining mustard mixture. Broil 5 to 6 minutes longer or until pork is slightly pink when cut near bone.

NUTRITION INFORMATION
1 Serving

Calories 165 (Calories from Fat 70)
Fat 8g (Saturated 3g)
Cholesterol 65mg
Sodium 70mg
Carbohydrate 1g (Dietary Fiber 0g)
Protein 22g

% DAILY VALUE: Vitamin A 0%; Vitamin C 0%; Calcium 0%; Iron 4%

DIET EXCHANGES: 3 Lean Meat

Cajun Mustard Pork Chops

rich honey-mustard pork medallions

LOW FAT / LOW CHOLESTEROL / LOW CALORIE

PREP: 10 min **MARINATE:** 15 min **COOK:** 8 min
4 SERVINGS

Pork has slimmed down! Once thought of as a fatty meat, pork today is leaner than it's ever been. For the leanest pork cut, choose the tenderloin.

1 pound pork tenderloin

2 tablespoons honey

1 tablespoon yellow mustard

1/4 teaspoon salt

1/4 teaspoon ground allspice

1/8 teaspoon ground red pepper (cayenne)

1/4 cup water

2 teaspoons firmly packed brown sugar

Remove fat from pork. Cut pork into 1/4-inch slices. Mix remaining ingredients except water and brown sugar in shallow glass or plastic bowl. Add pork; turn to coat with marinade. Cover and refrigerate 15 minutes. Mix water and brown sugar until sugar is dissolved; set aside.

Spray 10-inch nonstick skillet with cooking spray; heat over medium-high heat. Remove pork from marinade; discard marinade. Cook pork in skillet 5 to 6 minutes, turning once, until no longer pink. Remove pork from skillet; keep warm.

Reduce heat to low. Stir water mixture into drippings in skillet. Heat to boiling; stirring constantly. Boil and stir 1 minute. Drizzle sauce over pork.

NUTRITION INFORMATION
1 Serving

Calories 190 (Calories from Fat 45)
Fat 5g (Saturated 2g)
Cholesterol 70mg
Sodium 100mg
Carbohydrate 11g (Dietary Fiber 0g)
Protein 26g

% DAILY VALUE: Vitamin A 0%; Vitamin C 0%; Calcium 0%; Iron 8%

DIET EXCHANGES: 4 Very Lean Meat, 1/2 Fruit

raspberry-ginger pork skewers

LOW FAT / LOW CHOLESTEROL / LOW CALORIE

PREP: 20 min **BROIL:** 14 min
4 SERVINGS

For the brilliant yellow color of saffron rice at a fraction of the price, serve this dish with turmeric rice. Simply add 1/2 teaspoon ground turmeric to 1 cup uncooked plain white rice, and cook as directed on package.

1 pound pork tenderloin

1/2 cup raspberry spreadable fruit

1 tablespoon raspberry vinegar or red wine vinegar

1 teaspoon grated gingerroot

1/4 teaspoon salt

1/4 teaspoon ground red pepper (cayenne)

2 small red onions, cut into eighths

2 unpeeled oranges, cut into 1/2-inch slices and slices cut into fourths

Set oven control to broil. Remove fat from pork. Cut pork into 1-inch pieces. Beat spreadable fruit, vinegar, gingerroot, salt and red pepper with wire whisk until blended; set aside.

Thread pork, onions and oranges alternately on each of eight 10-inch metal skewers,* leaving space between each piece. Broil skewers with tops about 4 inches from heat 7 minutes, brushing frequently with glaze. Turn skewers; brush with glaze. Broil 6 to 7 minutes longer or until pork is no longer pink.

*If using bamboo skewers, soak in water at least 30 minutes before using to prevent burning.

NUTRITION INFORMATION
1 Serving

Calories 300 (Calories from Fat 45)
Fat 5g (Saturated 2g)
Cholesterol 70mg
Sodium 220mg
Carbohydrate 39g (Dietary Fiber 3g)
Protein 27g

% DAILY VALUE: Vitamin A 2%; Vitamin C 34%; Calcium 4%; Iron 10%

DIET EXCHANGES: 3 Very Lean Meat, 2 Vegetable, 2 Fruit

pork medallions with hot pineapple glaze

LOW FAT / LOW CHOLESTEROL / LOW CALORIE

PREP: 10 min **COOK:** 8 min
4 SERVINGS

This dish combines the best of both worlds—juicy pineapple sweetness with spicy-hot red pepper. For a cooling accompaniment, add a side of hot cooked rice or pasta and a bowl of fresh pineapple chunks topped with fresh mint.

1-pound pork tenderloin

1/4 teaspoon salt

1/3 cup pineapple or orange marmalade spreadable fruit

2 teaspoons Worcestershire sauce

2 teaspoons cider vinegar

1/2 teaspoon grated gingerroot

1/4 teaspoon crushed red pepper, if desired

Remove fat from pork. Cut pork into 1/4-inch slices. Sprinkle both sides of pork with salt.

Spray 12-inch nonstick skillet with cooking spray; heat over medium-high heat. Cook pork in skillet 5 to 6 minutes, turning once, until no longer pink. Remove pork from skillet; keep warm.

Mix remaining ingredients in skillet; heat to boiling. Boil and stir 1 minute. Serve sauce over pork.

NUTRITION INFORMATION
1 Serving

Calories 205 (Calories from Fat 35)
Fat 4g (Saturated 1g)
Cholesterol 65mg
Sodium 80mg
Carbohydrate 18g (Dietary Fiber 0g)
Protein 24g

% DAILY VALUE: Vitamin A 0%; Vitamin C 0%; Calcium 0%; Iron 8%

DIET EXCHANGES: 3 1/2 Very Lean Meat, 1 Fruit

Pork Medallions with Hot Pineapple Glaze

pork with caramelized onions

LOW FAT / LOW CHOLESTEROL / LOW CALORIE

PREP: 10 min **COOK:** 12 min
4 SERVINGS

1-pound pork tenderloin

1/2 teaspoon salt

1/4 teaspoon paprika

1 large onion, thinly sliced

1/4 teaspoon sugar

Remove fat from pork. Cut pork into 1/2-inch slices. Sprinkle salt and paprika over both sides of pork.

Spray 10-inch nonstick skillet with cooking spray; heat over medium-high. Cook pork in skillet 6 to 8 minutes, turning once, until no longer pink. Remove pork from skillet; keep warm.

Spray skillet with cooking spray; heat over medium-high heat. Cook onion in skillet 1 minute, stirring frequently. Reduce heat to medium. Stir in sugar. Cook about 3 minutes longer, stirring frequently, until onions are soft and golden brown. Spoon over pork.

NUTRITION INFORMATION
1 Serving

Calories 140 (Calories from Fat 55)
Fat 6g (Saturated 2g)
Cholesterol 50mg
Sodium 330mg
Carbohydrate 5g (Dietary Fiber 1g)
Protein 18g

% DAILY VALUE: Vitamin A 0%; Vitamin C 2%; Calcium 0%; Iron 4%

DIET EXCHANGES: 3 Very Lean Meat, 1 Vegetable

panfried ham with sweet balsamic-peach sauce

LOW FAT / LOW CHOLESTEROL / LOW CALORIE

PREP: 10 min **COOK:** 11 min
4 SERVINGS

1 pound fully cooked lower-fat, lower-sodium ham

1 bag (16 ounces) frozen sliced peaches, thawed and drained

1/4 cup raspberry spreadable fruit

2 tablespoons packed brown sugar

1 tablespoon balsamic vinegar

1/4 teaspoon crushed red pepper, if desired

Cut ham into 4 slices, each about 1/4 inch thick.

Spray 12-inch nonstick skillet with cooking spray; heat over medium-high. Heat remaining ingredients in skillet about 6 minutes, stirring frequently, until peaches are tender and sauce is reduced to a glaze.

Add ham; reduce heat to medium. Cover and cook about 5 minutes, turning once, until ham is hot.

NUTRITION INFORMATION
1 Serving

Calories 230 (Calories from Fat 30)
Fat 4g (Saturated 1g)
Cholesterol 50mg
Sodium 840mg
Carbohydrate 34g (Dietary Fiber 3g)
Protein 19g

% DAILY VALUE: Vitamin A 6%; Vitamin C 6%; Calcium 2%; Iron 8%

DIET EXCHANGES: 3 Very Lean Meat, 2 Fruit

loaded potatoes

LOW FAT / LOW CHOLESTEROL / LOW CALORIE

PREP: 15 min **COOK:** 5 min **STAND:** 5 min

4 SERVINGS

These quick-baked and moist potatoes overflow with layers and layers of flavor! Red potatoes are used because they contain more moisture than the drier, flakier russets, but you can use baking potatoes and still get the same great flavor.

4 medium unpeeled red potatoes

1 package (8 ounces) sliced mushrooms

3/4 cup chopped fully cooked lower-fat, lower-sodium ham

8 medium green onions, sliced (1/2 cup)

1/8 teaspoon ground red pepper (cayenne)

1/2 cup fat-free sour cream

1/2 cup shredded reduced-fat sharp Cheddar cheese (2 ounces)

Pierce potatoes with fork. Arrange potatoes about 1 inch apart in circle on microwavable paper towel. Microwave uncovered on High 8 to 10 minutes or until tender. (Or bake potatoes in 375° oven 1 to 1 1/2 hours.) Let potatoes stand until cool enough to handle.

Spray 4-quart Dutch oven with cooking spray; heat over medium-high heat. Cook mushrooms in Dutch oven 1 minute, stirring frequently; reduce heat to medium. Cover and cook 3 minutes; remove from heat. Stir in ham, onions and red pepper. Cover and let stand 5 minutes.

Split baked potatoes lengthwise in half; fluff with fork. Spread 1 tablespoon of the sour cream over each potato half. Top with ham mixture and cheese.

NUTRITION INFORMATION
1 Serving

Calories 245 (Calories from Fat 65)
Fat 7g (Saturated 4g)
Cholesterol 35mg
Sodium 480mg
Carbohydrate 31g (Dietary Fiber 3g)
Protein 17g

% DAILY VALUE: Vitamin A 8%; Vitamin C 14%; Calcium 14%; Iron 10%

DIET EXCHANGES: 2 Starch, 1 Medium-Fat Meat, 1 Fat

Loaded Potatoes

farmhouse ham chowder

LOW FAT / LOW CHOLESTEROL / LOW CALORIE

PREP: 10 min **COOK:** 20 min
6 SERVINGS

2 medium potatoes, cut into 1/2-inch pieces

1 medium red bell pepper, chopped (1 cup)

1 bag (16 ounces) frozen broccoli, carrots and cauliflower (or other combination)

1 cup chopped fully cooked lower-fat, lower-sodium ham

1/4 cup water

1/2 teaspoon dried thyme leaves

1 can (12 ounces) evaporated fat-free milk

1/2 cup fat-free (skim) milk

3/4 teaspoon salt

3 ounces fat-free process cheese product loaf, diced

1/8 teaspoon ground red pepper (cayenne)

1/4 cup chopped fresh parsley

Mix potatoes, bell pepper, frozen vegetables, ham, water and thyme in 3-quart saucepan. Heat to boiling, stirring occasionally; reduce heat to low. Cover and simmer about 15 minutes, stirring occasionally, until potatoes are just tender.

Stir in remaining ingredients except ground red pepper and parsley. Simmer uncovered, stirring occasionally, until cheese is melted. Stir in ground red pepper. Sprinkle with parsley.

NUTRITION INFORMATION
1 Serving

Calories 170 (Calories from Fat 20)
Fat 2g (Saturated 1g)
Cholesterol 15mg
Sodium 870mg
Carbohydrate 26g (Dietary Fiber 4g)
Protein 16g

% DAILY VALUE: Vitamin A 52%; Vitamin C 58%; Calcium 34%; Iron 10%

DIET EXCHANGES: 1 Starch, 1 Very Lean Meat 1 Vegetable, 1/2 Skim Milk

honey ham & black-eyed pea salad

LOW FAT / LOW CHOLESTEROL / LOW CALORIE

PREP: 15 min **CHILL:** 1 hr

4 SERVINGS

Their name is a misnomer. Black-eyed peas are really beans, and what a fiber-full bean bargain they are! One cup of these gems contains 11 grams of fiber and only 1 gram of fat.

1/2 cup diced lean honey ham

1/2 cup finely chopped red onion

4 medium roma (plum) tomatoes, chopped (1 1/3 cups)

1 medium stalk celery, finely chopped (1/2 cup)

1 small red bell pepper, chopped (1/2 cup)

1/4 cup cider vinegar

1 tablespoon olive or vegetable oil

1 teaspoon sugar

1/4 teaspoon dried thyme leaves

1/8 teaspoon red pepper sauce

1 can (15 ounces) black-eyed peas, rinsed and drained

Mix all ingredients except peas in large glass or plastic bowl. Cover and refrigerate 1 hour to blend flavors. Just before serving, stir in peas.

NUTRITION INFORMATION
1 Serving

Calories 200 (Calories from Fat 55)
Fat 6g (Saturated 1g)
Cholesterol 15mg
Sodium 580mg
Carbohydrate 31g (Dietary Fiber 9g)
Protein 15g

% DAILY VALUE: Vitamin A 14%; Vitamin C 84%; Calcium 4%; Iron 20%

DIET EXCHANGES: 1 Starch, 1 Lean Meat, 3 Vegetable

IS OLIVE OIL BETTER FOR YOU?

True or false? A healthy diet means one that is similar to that of the Mediterranean region, using plenty of olive oil.

ANSWER: False. While it is true that olive oil may be helpful in reducing the level of "bad" low-density lipoprotein cholesterol (LDL) and maintaining the "good" high-density lipoprotein cholesterol level (HDL) in our blood, it still is not something that you should plan on eating in large quantities. Thought to be a culprit in heart disease, LDL contains most of the cholesterol found in the blood and is associated with making cholesterol available for cell structures, hormones and nerve coverings. LDL also deposits cholesterol on artery walls. HDLs on the other hand, help to remove cholesterol from body tissues and blood and return it to the liver to be used again. This recycling process has earned HDL the "good" cholesterol label.

Regardless of what experts tell us about this golden oil pressed from olives, it's still 100 percent fat, so it supplies the same amount of fat and calories as butter, margarine or other oils. Just the makeup of the fatty acids is different.

countryside pasta toss

LOW FAT / LOW CHOLESTEROL / LOW CALORIE

PREP: 10 min **COOK:** 12 min
4 SERVINGS

1 cup uncooked rotini pasta (3 ounces)

3/4 pound new potatoes, cut into 1/2-inch wedges

1 cup frozen broccoli flowerets

1 cup frozen baby-cut carrots, thawed and drained

1/2 cup fresh or frozen snap pea pods

1 tablespoon margarine

2 tablespoons chopped fresh parsley

1 teaspoon dried dill weed

1/2 teaspoon salt

2 ounces fully cooked lower-fat, lower-sodium ham, cut into thin strips

Cook and drain pasta as directed on package. While pasta is cooking, place steamer basket in 1/2 inch water in 3-quart saucepan (water should not touch bottom of saucepan). Place potatoes, broccoli and carrots in basket. Cover tightly and heat to boiling; reduce heat to medium-low. Steam 5 minutes. Add pea pods. Cover and steam about 2 minutes longer or until potatoes are tender.

Place vegetables in medium bowl. Add margarine, parsley, dill weed and salt; toss until coated. Stir in ham and pasta; toss.

NUTRITION INFORMATION
1 Serving

Calories 240 (Calories from Fat 35)
Fat 4g (Saturated 1g)
Cholesterol 5mg
Sodium 230mg
Carbohydrate 47g (Dietary Fiber 6g)
Protein 10g

% DAILY VALUE: Vitamin A 100%; Vitamin C 28%; Calcium 6%; Iron 16%

DIET EXCHANGES: 2 Starch, 3 Vegetable

Countryside Pasta Toss

lamb with creamy mint sauce

LOW FAT / LOW CHOLESTEROL / LOW CALORIE

PREP: 5 min **BROIL:** 14 min
4 SERVINGS

2/3 cup plain fat-free yogurt

1/4 cup firmly packed fresh mint leaves

2 tablespoons sugar

4 lamb loin chops, about 1 inch thick (1 pound)

Place yogurt, mint and sugar in blender or food processor. Cover and blend on medium speed, stopping blender occasionally to scrape sides, until leaves are finely chopped.

Set oven control to broil. Spray broiler-pan rack with cooking spray. Remove fat from lamb. Place lamb on rack in broiler pan. Broil with tops 2 to 3 inches from heat 12 to 14 minutes, turning after 6 minutes, until meat thermometer reads 160° (medium doneness). Serve with sauce.

NUTRITION INFORMATION
1 Serving

Calories 175 (Calories from Fat 55)
Fat 6g (Saturated 2g)
Cholesterol 60mg
Sodium 75mg
Carbohydrate 10g (Dietary Fiber 0g)
Protein 20g

% DAILY VALUE: Vitamin A 2%; Vitamin C 4%; Calcium 8%; Iron 8%

DIET EXCHANGES: 2 Lean Meat, 1/2 Fruit, 1/2 Skim Milk

mustard lamb chops

LOW FAT / LOW CHOLESTEROL / LOW CALORIE

PREP: 10 min **BROIL:** 11 min
6 SERVINGS

6 lamb sirloin or shoulder chops, about 3/4 inch thick (about 2 pounds)

1 tablespoon chopped fresh or 1 teaspoon dried thyme leaves

2 tablespoons Dijon mustard

1/4 teaspoon salt

Set oven control to broil. Remove fat from lamb. Place lamb on rack in broiler pan. Mix remaining ingredients. Brush half of the mustard mixture evenly over lamb.

Broil lamb with tops 3 to 4 inches from heat about 4 minutes or until brown. Turn lamb; brush with remaining mustard mixture. Broil 5 to 7 minutes longer for medium doneness (160°).

NUTRITION INFORMATION
1 Serving

Calories 115 (Calories from Fat 65)
Fat 7g (Saturated 3g)
Cholesterol 70mg
Sodium 220mg
Carbohydrate 0g (Dietary Fiber 0g)
Protein 22g

% DAILY VALUE: Vitamin A 2%; Vitamin C 0%; Calcium 2%; Iron 12%

DIET EXCHANGES: 3 Lean Meat

low fat

Main-dish recipes have 10 or fewer grams of fat per serving.

Low-fat side dishes and desserts have 3 or fewer grams of fat per serving.

low cholesterol

Recipes have 90 or fewer milligrams of cholesterol per serving.

low calorie

Recipes have 350 or fewer calories per serving with the exception of desserts.

Low-calorie desserts have 250 or fewer calories per serving.

CHAPTER 4

meatless main dishes

Gorgonzola Rigatoni with Vegetables (page 124)

gorgonzola rigatoni with vegetables

LOW FAT / LOW CHOLESTEROL

PREP: 10 min **COOK:** 15 min
4 SERVINGS

Gorgonzola cheese proves the old adage that a little goes a long way! Its strong and tangy flavor packs a tasty punch without adding a lot of fat and calories. You can also try blue cheese or feta cheese in this recipe.

3 cups uncooked rigatoni pasta (9 ounces)

2 cups broccoli flowerets

1 tablespoon cornstarch

1 can (12 ounces) evaporated fat-free milk

1/2 cup crumbled Gorgonzola cheese (2 ounces)

1 small tomato, chopped (1/2 cup)

1 can (6 ounces) sliced mushrooms, drained

10 pitted ripe olives, cut in half

1/2 teaspoon salt

1/4 teaspoon pepper

Oregano sprigs, if desired

Cook and drain pasta as directed on package. While pasta is cooking, place steamer basket in 1/2 inch water in saucepan or skillet (water should not touch bottom of basket). Place broccoli in basket. Cover tightly and heat to boiling; reduce heat to medium-low. Steam about 3 minutes or until crisp-tender.

Mix cornstarch and milk in 3-quart saucepan. Heat to boiling over medium heat, stirring constantly; reduce heat to low. Stir in Gorgonzola cheese; continue stirring 2 to 3 minutes or until cheese is melted.

Stir broccoli, tomato, mushrooms, olives, salt and pepper into cheese sauce; heat through. Serve over pasta. Garnish with oregano.

NUTRITION INFORMATION
1 Serving

Calories 435 (Calories from Fat 65)
Fat 7g (Saturated 3g)
Cholesterol 10mg
Sodium 830mg
Carbohydrate 79g (Dietary Fiber 6g)
Protein 20g

% DAILY VALUE: Vitamin A 16%; Vitamin C 38%; Calcium 26%; Iron 24%

DIET EXCHANGES: 4 Starch, 4 Vegetable, 1/2 Fat

LOW-FAT COOKING 101: SIMPLE STEAMING METHODS

Steaming is a great way to keep the vitamins and minerals from leaking out of your food. Because steaming requires no added fat for cooking, it's an ideal technique for healthy cooking.

Collapsible metal steamers are a great tool. They take up little storage space and will expand to fit almost any pot or skillet. When placing the steamer in the pot, be sure the water does not touch the bottom of the steamer basket.

Bamboo steamers look like a covered basket with a flat bottom that fit inside a wok or over a medium skillet filled with simmering water. These stackable steamers are ideal for steaming a wide variety of vegetables, all at the same time. Place longer-cooking vegetables in a steamer basket closest to the heat, and place shorter-cooking items near the top. Search out bamboo steamers in houseware departments or in Asian cookware shops.

If you don't have a steamer, don't despair! You can improvise by using a strainer or a footed colander.

easy mac 'n' cheese

LOW FAT / LOW CHOLESTEROL / LOW CALORIE

PREP: 10 min **COOK:** 12 min
4 SERVINGS

1 package (7 ounces) macaroni shells (2 cups)

1 tablespoon margarine

2 tablespoons all-purpose flour

1/4 teaspoon salt

1/4 teaspoon ground mustard

1/8 teaspoon pepper

1 cup fat-free (skim) milk

1 cup shredded reduced-fat Cheddar cheese (4 ounces)

2 tablespoons chopped red bell pepper

1 medium green onion, sliced (1 tablespoon)

Cook and drain macaroni as directed on package. While macaroni is cooking, melt margarine in 3-quart nonstick saucepan over low heat. Stir in flour, salt, mustard and pepper. Cook over low heat, stirring constantly, until margarine is absorbed; remove from heat.

Gradually stir milk into flour mixture. Heat to boiling, stirring constantly. Boil and stir 1 minute. Stir in cheese until melted.

Stir macaroni, bell pepper and onion into sauce. Cook, stirring constantly, until hot.

NUTRITION INFORMATION
1 Serving

Calories 295 (Calories from Fat 55)
Fat 6g (Saturated 2g)
Cholesterol 5mg
Sodium 390mg
Carbohydrate 46g (Dietary Fiber 2g)
Protein 16g

% DAILY VALUE: Vitamin A 12%; Vitamin C 8%; Calcium 20%; Iron 12%

DIET EXCHANGES: 3 Starch, 1 Lean Meat

Easy Mac 'n' Cheese

roasted red pepper mostaccioli

LOW FAT / LOW CHOLESTEROL / LOW CALORIE

PREP: 10 min **COOK:** 20 min
6 SERVINGS

Rev up your taste buds with roasted red peppers. Jars of these jewels can be found in the condiment section of most super-markets. Because the peppers are packed in oil, be sure to drain them well before using.

3 cups uncooked mostaccioli pasta (9 ounces)

1 can (14 1/2 ounces) Italian-style stewed tomatoes, undrained

1 jar (7 ounces) roasted red bell peppers, drained

1 tablespoon olive or vegetable oil

1 clove garlic, finely chopped

2 teaspoons chopped fresh or 1/2 teaspoon dried oregano leaves

2 teaspoons capers

Freshly ground pepper, if desired

Cook and drain pasta as directed on package. While pasta is cooking, place tomatoes and bell peppers in blender or food processor. Cover and blend on high speed until smooth.

Heat oil in 1-quart nonstick saucepan over medium heat. Cook garlic in oil, stirring occasionally, until golden. Stir in tomato mixture, oregano and capers. Simmer uncovered 15 minutes, stirring occasionally. Serve over pasta with pepper.

NUTRITION INFORMATION
1 Serving

Calories 205 (Calories from Fat 25)
Fat 3g (Saturated 0g)
Cholesterol 0mg
Sodium 220mg
Carbohydrate 41g (Dietary Fiber 3g)
Protein 6g

% DAILY VALUE: Vitamin A 14%; Vitamin C 54%; Calcium 2%; Iron 12%

DIET EXCHANGES: 2 Starch, 2 Vegetable

portabella gemelli

LOW FAT / LOW CHOLESTEROL

PREP: 10 min **COOK:** 15 min
4 SERVINGS

3 cups uncooked gemelli (twist) pasta
(6 ounces)

2 packages (6 ounces each) sliced fresh
portabella mushrooms

1 1/4 cups water

2 tablespoons fat-free (skim) milk

1 tablespoon plus 1 teaspoon cornstarch

1 tablespoon chopped fresh or 1 teaspoon
dried basil leaves

2 teaspoons chopped fresh or 3/4 teaspoon
dried oregano leaves

1/2 teaspoon chopped fresh or 1/8 teaspoon
dried rosemary leaves, crumbled

1 1/2 teaspoons beef bouillon granules

2 teaspoons Dijon mustard

1/4 teaspoon salt

Cook and drain pasta as directed on package. While pasta is cooking, spray 12-inch nonstick skillet with cooking spray; heat over medium heat. Cook mushrooms in skillet about 8 minutes, stirring occasionally, until tender. Remove mushrooms from skillet; set aside.

Beat remaining ingredients with wire whisk until blended; add to skillet. Heat to boiling, stirring constantly. Boil and stir 1 minute.

Stir mushrooms with any liquid into sauce; reduce heat to low. Cook about 2 minutes until sauce is slightly thickened; remove from heat. Serve over pasta.

NUTRITION INFORMATION
1 Serving

Calories 355 (Calories from Fat 20)
Fat 2g (Saturated 0g)
Cholesterol 0mg
Sodium 520mg
Carbohydrate 74g (Dietary Fiber 4g)
Protein 14g

% DAILY VALUE: Vitamin A 0%; Vitamin C 2%; Calcium 4%; Iron 24%

DIET EXCHANGES: 4 Starch, 3 Vegetable

mediterranean couscous

LOW FAT / LOW CHOLESTEROL / LOW CALORIE

PREP: 15 min **COOK:** 5 min **STAND:** 5 min
4 SERVINGS

2 teaspoons margarine

4 medium green onions, chopped (1/4 cup)

1 clove garlic, finely chopped

1 1/2 cups water

1/2 teaspoon chicken bouillon granules

1 cup uncooked couscous

1/4 cup chopped fresh parsley

1 tablespoon chopped fresh or 1/2 teaspoon dried basil leaves

1/4 teaspoon pepper

1 medium yellow summer squash, chopped (1 cup)

1 medium tomato, chopped (3/4 cup)

Melt margarine in 2-quart nonstick saucepan over medium-high heat. Cook onions and garlic in margarine, stirring frequently, until onions are tender. Stir in water and bouillon granules. Heat to boiling; remove from heat.

Stir in remaining ingredients. Cover and let stand about 5 minutes or until liquid is absorbed. Fluff lightly with fork.

NUTRITION INFORMATION
1 Serving

Calories 180 (Calories from Fat 20)
Fat 2g (Saturated 0g)
Cholesterol 0mg
Sodium 200mg
Carbohydrate 37g (Dietary Fiber 3g)
Protein 7g

% DAILY VALUE: Vitamin A 8%; Vitamin C 28%; Calcium 2%; Iron 6%

DIET EXCHANGES: 2 Starch, 1 Vegetable

Mediterranean Couscous

vegetable manicotti

LOW FAT / LOW CHOLESTEROL / LOW CALORIE

PREP: 25 min **BAKE:** 45 min
4 SERVINGS

8 uncooked manicotti shells

1 teaspoon olive or vegetable oil

1 medium carrot, shredded (1/2 cup)

1/2 cup shredded zucchini

1/2 cup sliced mushrooms (1 1/2 ounces)

4 medium green onions, sliced (1/4 cup)

1 clove garlic, finely chopped

1/4 cup grated reduced-fat or fat-free Parmesan cheese topping

1/4 cup fat-free cholesterol-free egg product or 2 egg whites

2 tablespoons chopped fresh or 2 teaspoons dried basil leaves

1 container (15 ounces) fat-free ricotta cheese

1 can (8 ounces) tomato sauce

1/2 cup shredded low-fat mozzarella cheese (2 ounces)

Heat oven to 350°. Spray rectangular baking dish, 11 × 7 × 1 1/2 inches, with cooking spray. Cook and drain manicotti as directed on package.

While manicotti is cooking, heat oil in 10-inch nonstick skillet over medium-high heat. Cook carrot, zucchini, mushrooms, onions and garlic in oil, stirring frequently, until vegetables are crisp-tender. Stir in remaining ingredients except tomato sauce and mozzarella cheese.

Pour 1/3 cup of the tomato sauce into baking dish. Fill manicotti shells with vegetable mixture; place in baking dish. Pour remaining tomato sauce over manicotti. Sprinkle with mozzarella cheese. Cover and bake 40 to 45 minutes or until hot and bubbly.

NUTRITION INFORMATION
1 Serving

Calories 315 (Calories from Fat 45)
Fat 5g (Saturated 2g)
Cholesterol 10mg
Sodium 640mg
Carbohydrate 44g (Dietary Fiber 4g)
Protein 27g

% DAILY VALUE: Vitamin A 18%; Vitamin C 10%; Calcium 36%; Iron 14%

DIET EXCHANGES: 1 Starch, 1 Lean Meat, 3 Vegetable, 1 Skim Milk

mushroom & mozzarella risotto

LOW FAT / LOW CHOLESTEROL / LOW CALORIE

PREP: 10 min **COOK:** 35 min
6 SERVINGS

2 cups chopped mushrooms (8 ounces)

2 large onions, chopped (2 cups)

2 cups uncooked Arborio rice or regular medium-grain white rice

2 cups white wine or apple juice

5 1/2 to 6 cups fat-free reduced-sodium chicken or vegetable broth, heated

1/2 cup shredded low-fat mozzarella cheese (2 ounces)

2 tablespoons grated reduced-fat or fat-free Parmesan cheese topping

2 tablespoons chopped fresh chives

Spray 3-quart saucepan with cooking spray; heat over medium heat. Cook mushrooms and onions in saucepan about 5 minutes, stirring occasionally, until onions are tender. Stir in rice. Cook 3 minutes, stirring constantly.

Stir in wine and 2 cups of the broth. Heat to boiling; reduce heat to medium. Cook uncovered about 5 minutes, stirring occasionally, until most liquid is absorbed.

Stir in 1 cup of the broth. Cook uncovered, stirring occasionally, until most liquid is absorbed. Repeat with remaining broth, 1 cup at a time, until rice is tender and mixture is slightly thickened. Stir in remaining ingredients.

NUTRITION INFORMATION
1 Serving

Calories 325 (Calories from Fat 25)
Fat 3g (Saturated 1g)
Cholesterol 5mg
Sodium 330mg
Carbohydrate 69g (Dietary Fiber 2g)
Protein 9g

% DAILY VALUE: Vitamin A 16%; Vitamin C 4%; Calcium 12%; Iron 16%

DIET EXCHANGES: 4 Starch, 1 Vegetable

steamed chinese vegetables with brown rice

LOW FAT / LOW CHOLESTEROL / LOW CALORIE

PREP: 20 min **COOK:** 10 min
4 SERVINGS

Bok choy is a versatile mild vegetable that resembles a bunch of wide-stalked celery with long, full leaves. You can easily substitute 1 cup sliced celery for the bok choy in this recipe.

1 Japanese or regular eggplant (1 1/2 pounds), cut into 2 × 1/2-inch strips (3 cups)

1 medium red bell pepper, cut into julienne strips (1 1/2 cups)

1 large carrot, cut into julienne strips (1 cup)

1 cup sliced bok choy (stems and leaves)

1 medium onion, thinly sliced

1/2 pound snow (Chinese) pea pods (2 cups)

2 tablespoons soy sauce

1 tablespoon creamy peanut butter

1 tablespoon hoisin sauce

1 teaspoon grated gingerroot

1 clove garlic, finely chopped

2 cups hot cooked brown rice

Place steamer basket in 1/2 inch water in saucepan or skillet (water should not touch bottom of basket). Place eggplant, bell pepper, carrot, bok choy and onion in steamer basket. Cover tightly and heat to boiling; reduce heat to medium-low. Steam 5 to 8 minutes, adding pea pods for the last minute of steaming, until vegetables are crisp-tender.

Beat soy sauce, peanut butter, hoisin sauce, gingerroot and garlic in large bowl with wire whisk until blended. Add vegetables; toss. Serve over rice.

NUTRITION INFORMATION
1 Serving

Calories 190 (Calories from Fat 35)
Fat 4g (Saturated 1g)
Cholesterol 0mg
Sodium 570mg
Carbohydrate 38g (Dietary Fiber 6g)
Protein 7g

% DAILY VALUE: Vitamin A 50%; Vitamin C 68%; Calcium 6%; Iron 10%

DIET EXCHANGES: 2 Starch, 2 Vegetable

Steamed Chinese Vegetables with Brown Rice

indian lentils & rice

LOW FAT / LOW CHOLESTEROL / LOW CALORIE

PREP: 15 min **COOK:** 40 min
6 SERVINGS

Yogurt is a terrific addition to Indian foods, plus many brands of yogurt contain live and active cultures that can help keep your digestive system healthy. Check the container label for the "live and active cultures" seal.

4 medium green onions, chopped (1/4 cup)

1 tablespoon finely chopped gingerroot

1/8 teaspoon crushed red pepper

2 cloves garlic, finely chopped

1 can (49 1/2 ounces) or 3 cans (14 1/2 ounces each) vegetable broth

1 1/2 cups dried lentils (12 ounces), sorted and rinsed

1 teaspoon ground turmeric

1/2 teaspoon salt

1 large tomato, chopped (1 cup)

1/4 cup shredded coconut

2 tablespoons chopped fresh or 2 teaspoons dried mint leaves

3 cups hot cooked rice

1 1/2 cups plain fat-free yogurt

Spray 3-quart saucepan with cooking spray. Cook onions, gingerroot, red pepper and garlic in saucepan over medium heat 3 to 5 minutes, stirring occasionally, until onions are tender.

Stir in 5 cups of the broth, the lentils, turmeric and salt. Heat to boiling; reduce heat to low. Cover and simmer 25 to 30 minutes, adding remaining broth if needed, until lentils are tender. Stir in tomato, coconut and mint. Serve over rice with yogurt.

NUTRITION INFORMATION
1 Serving

Calories 285 (Calories from Fat 20)
Fat 2g (Saturated 1g)
Cholesterol 0mg
Sodium 820mg
Carbohydrate 61g (Dietary Fiber 12g)
Protein 18g

% DAILY VALUE: Vitamin A 20%; Vitamin C 10%; Calcium 18%; Iron 32%

DIET EXCHANGES: 4 Starch

polenta squares with tomato-basil sauce

LOW FAT / LOW CHOLESTEROL / LOW CALORIE

PREP: 20 min **CHILL:** 1 hr **BROIL:** 6 min

4 SERVINGS

1 cup yellow cornmeal

1 cup fat-free vegetable or chicken broth

3 cups boiling water

1/2 teaspoon salt

2 tablespoons grated reduced-fat or fat-free Parmesan cheese topping

Cooking spray

1 cup reduced-fat spaghetti sauce

2 tablespoons chopped fresh or 1 teaspoon dried basil leaves

1/2 cup shredded low-fat mozzarella cheese (2 ounces)

Mix cornmeal and broth in 2-quart saucepan. Stir in boiling water and salt. Cook over medium-high heat, stirring constantly, until mixture thickens and boils; reduce heat to low. Cover and simmer 10 minutes, stirring frequently; remove from heat. Stir in Parmesan cheese.

Spray square pan, 8 × 8 × 2 inches, with cooking spray. Spread polenta in pan. Cover and refrigerate about 1 hour or until firm. Cut into 4 squares.

Set oven control to broil. Line broiler pan with aluminum foil. Spray both sides of polenta squares with cooking spray; place in broiler pan. Broil with tops of polenta about 4 inches from heat about 2 minutes each side or until light brown.

Spoon spaghetti sauce over polenta in pan. Sprinkle with basil and mozzarella cheese. Broil about 2 minutes or until cheese is melted.

NUTRITION INFORMATION
1 Serving

Calories 230 (Calories from Fat 45)
Fat 5g (Saturated 2g)
Cholesterol 10mg
Sodium 690mg
Carbohydrate 42g (Dietary Fiber 4g)
Protein 8g

% DAILY VALUE: Vitamin A 12%; Vitamin C 8%; Calcium 14%; Iron 10%

DIET EXCHANGES: 2 Starch, 2 Vegetable, 1/2 Fat

creamy quinoa primavera

LOW FAT / LOW CHOLESTEROL / LOW CALORIE

PREP: 15 min **COOK:** 20 min
6 SERVINGS

Quinoa ("keen-wa") was once a staple food of the Incan civilization in Peru. It is a small grain with a soft crunch and can be used in any recipe calling for rice. Be sure to rinse it well before using to remove the bitter-tasting, naturally occurring saponin (nature's insect repellent) that forms on the outside of the kernel.

1 1/2 cups uncooked quinoa

3 cups fat-free vegetable or chicken broth

2 ounces reduced-fat cream cheese (Neufchâtel)

1 tablespoon chopped fresh or 1 teaspoon dried basil leaves

2 teaspoons margarine

2 cloves garlic, finely chopped

5 cups thinly sliced or bite-size pieces assorted vegetables (asparagus, bell pepper, broccoli, carrots, zucchini)

2 tablespoons shredded Romano cheese

Rinse quinoa thoroughly; drain. Heat quinoa and broth to boiling in 2-quart saucepan; reduce heat to low. Cover and simmer 10 to 15 minutes or until all broth is absorbed. Stir in cream cheese and basil.

Melt margarine in 10-inch nonstick skillet over medium-high heat. Cook garlic in margarine about 30 seconds, stirring frequently, until golden. Stir in vegetables. Cook about 2 minutes, stirring frequently, until vegetables are crisp-tender. Toss vegetables and quinoa mixture. Sprinkle with Romano cheese.

NUTRITION INFORMATION
1 Serving

Calories 235 (Calories from Fat 65)
Fat 7g (Saturated 2g)
Cholesterol 10mg
Sodium 630mg
Carbohydrate 36g (Dietary Fiber 5g)
Protein 12g

% DAILY VALUE: Vitamin A 48%; Vitamin C 22%; Calcium 8%; Iron 26%

DIET EXCHANGES: 2 Starch, 1 Vegetable, 1 Fat

GRAIN'S GOODNESS

Whole grains have a lot to offer for heart health. Take a look:

Fiber

Some grains, such as oats, barley, corn and rye, are good sources of soluble fiber, which research shows can help lower blood cholesterol levels.

Folic Acid

Whole-grain foods can be a great source of folic acid, a vitamin researchers believe may help reduce the risk for heart disease. Folic acid helps break down and neutralize homocysteine, a substance produced when your body digests protein. Scientists believe a buildup of homocysteine may injure arteries and allow for the accumulation of cholesterol and plaque inside them.

Antioxidants

Whole grains contain vitamin E, selenium and flavonoids, also known as antioxidants. These nutrients protect cells from being damaged by free radicals, which are substances that can make cholesterol more likely to build up inside arteries.

Good Sources of Whole Grains

- Barley
- Breads (whole wheat, rye and oat)
- Brown rice
- Cereals (whole-grain and whole wheat)
- Corn
- Quinoa
- Whole wheat pasta

Creamy Quinoa Primavera

mushroom-curry bulgur

LOW FAT / LOW CHOLESTEROL / LOW CALORIE

PREP: 6 min **COOK:** 15 min **STAND:** 20 min
4 SERVINGS

Bulgur, also spelled *bulgar*, is whole wheat that has been cooked, dried and then broken into coarse fragments. It's different from cracked wheat in that it is precooked. Bulgur supplies many needed minerals, such as phosphorous, potassium and iron.

3 cups sliced mushrooms (8 ounces)

2 large onions, chopped (2 cups)

2 cloves garlic, finely chopped

3 cups frozen green peas, red bell pepper and broccoli (or other combination)

1 1/2 cups uncooked bulgur

1/4 cup currants or raisins

2 teaspoons curry powder

1/2 teaspoon salt

2 cups water

Spray 10-inch nonstick skillet with cooking spray; heat over medium-high heat. Cook mushrooms, onions and garlic in skillet about 8 minutes, stirring occasionally, until onions are tender.

Stir in remaining ingredients except water. Cook 2 minutes, stirring occasionally. Stir in water. Heat to boiling; remove from heat. Cover and let stand 15 to 20 minutes or until water is absorbed.

NUTRITION INFORMATION
1 Serving

Calories 255 (Calories from Fat 10)
Fat 1g (Saturated 0g)
Cholesterol 0mg
Sodium 350mg
Carbohydrate 65g (Dietary Fiber 16g)
Protein 12g

% DAILY VALUE: Vitamin A 28%; Vitamin C 76%; Calcium 8%; Iron 18%

DIET EXCHANGES: 3 Starch, 1 Vegetable, 1 Fruit

cheesy soy burgers

LOW FAT / LOW CHOLESTEROL / LOW CALORIE

PREP: 15 min **COOK:** 10 min
4 SERVINGS

If soybeans are missing from your supermarket shelves, canned pinto beans, rinsed and drained, are a tasty bean backup.

1 can (15 ounces) soybeans, rinsed and drained

1/2 cup shredded fat-free Cheddar cheese (2 ounces)

1/4 cup dry bread crumbs

2 medium green onions, finely chopped (2 tablespoons)

1 teaspoon Worcestershire sauce

1/4 teaspoon pepper

1/8 teaspoon salt

2 tablespoons fat-free cholesterol-free egg product or 1 egg white

4 hamburger buns, split and toasted

Horseradish Sauce (above)

4 slices tomato

4 lettuce leaves

Mash beans in medium bowl. Mix in cheese, bread crumbs, onions, Worcestershire sauce, pepper, salt and egg product. Shape mixture into 4 patties.

Spray 10-inch nonstick skillet with cooking spray. Cook patties in skillet over medium heat about 10 minutes, turning once, until light brown. Serve on buns with Horseradish Sauce, tomato and lettuce.

Horseradish Sauce

1/2 cup plain fat-free yogurt

2 teaspoons prepared horseradish

Mix ingredients. Cover and refrigerate until ready to use.

SUPER SOY

The term *super* fits. Soy is showing promise on all sorts of health-promoting fronts. It may protect against heart disease, cancer and osteoporosis, and it may ease the hot flashes that accompany menopause, too. Pretty impressive credentials for a bean the size of a pearl.

Soy gets its health-enhancing status from a powerful little plant nutrient called isoflavone, which acts as an antioxidant and a cholesterol-reducer. Soy protein also plays an important role in lowering cholesterol. When soy protein replaces animal protein, such as meat, in the diet, studies have found that blood cholesterol levels can drop. Not only has soy reduced total blood cholesterol, it can also lower LDLs (the artery-clogging cholesterol) and slightly raise HDLs (the "good" cholesterol that can remove plaque from the arteries).

Good sources of soy include soy milk, roasted soy nuts, tofu, soy protein powder, soy protein bars, soy flour, soybeans, tempeh (a combination of fermented soybeans and grains) and miso (fermented soybean paste).

NUTRITION INFORMATION
1 Serving

Calories 305 (Calories from Fat 35)
Fat 4g (Saturated 0g)
Cholesterol 5mg
Sodium 530mg
Carbohydrate 59g (Dietary Fiber 11g)
Protein 19g

% DAILY VALUE: Vitamin A 6%; Vitamin C 10%; Calcium 24%; Iron 30%

DIET EXCHANGES: 4 Starch

layered enchilada bake

LOW FAT / LOW CHOLESTEROL / LOW CALORIE

PREP: 15 min **BAKE:** 30 min
4 SERVINGS

Green salsa, or *salsa verde*, is a combination of tomatillos (a small green cousin of the tomato with a tangy flavor), green chilies and cilantro. If you can't find green salsa, use tomato salsa instead. For a festive touch, garnish with whole chilies.

1 cup fat-free refried beans

1 can (4 ounces) chopped green chilies

1 small tomato, chopped (1/2 cup)

4 corn tortillas (5 or 6 inches in diameter)

1 1/4 cups green salsa (salsa verde)

1 1/2 cups shredded reduced-fat Cheddar cheese (6 ounces)

Fat-free sour cream, if desired

Heat oven to 350°. Spray pie plate, 9 × 1 1/4 inches, with cooking spray. Mix beans, chilies and tomato. Place 1 tortilla in pie plate. Layer with one-fourth each of the bean mixture, green salsa and cheese. Repeat 3 times.

Cover loosely and bake 25 to 30 minutes or until cheese is melted and beans are heated through. Serve with sour cream.

NUTRITION INFORMATION
1 Serving

Calories 190 (Calories from Fat 35)
Fat 4g (Saturated 2g)
Cholesterol 10mg
Sodium 770mg
Carbohydrate 28g (Dietary Fiber 6g)
Protein 16g

% DAILY VALUE: Vitamin A 10%; Vitamin C 30%; Calcium 26%; Iron 12%

DIET EXCHANGES: 1 Starch, 1 Lean Meat, 2 Vegetable

Layered Enchilada Bake

vegetarian shepherd's pie

LOW FAT / LOW CHOLESTEROL / LOW CALORIE

PREP: 10 min **COOK:** 23 min
6 SERVINGS

2 cans (15 or 16 ounces each) kidney beans, rinsed and drained

1 jar (16 ounces) thick-and-chunky salsa (2 cups)

1 cup frozen whole kernel corn

1 medium carrot, chopped (1/2 cup)

1 1/2 cups warm mashed potatoes

2 tablespoons grated reduced-fat or fat-free Parmesan cheese topping

Chopped fresh chives or parsley, if desired

Heat beans, salsa, corn and carrot to boiling in 10-inch nonstick skillet; reduce heat to low. Cover and simmer about 15 minutes or until carrot is tender.

Spoon mashed potatoes onto bean mixture around edge of skillet. Cover and simmer 5 minutes. Sprinkle with cheese and chives.

NUTRITION INFORMATION
1 Serving

Calories 240 (Calories from Fat 20)
Fat 2g (Saturated 0g)
Cholesterol 0mg
Sodium 650mg
Carbohydrate 51g (Dietary Fiber 12g)
Protein 16g

% DAILY VALUE: Vitamin A 22%; Vitamin C 18%; Calcium 10%; Iron 28%

DIET EXCHANGES: 3 Starch, 1 Vegetable

Vegetarian Shepherd's Pie

mexican black beans with cilantro-chili sour cream

LOW FAT / LOW CHOLESTEROL / LOW CALORIE

PREP: 10 min **COOK:** 2 min

4 SERVINGS

Rinsing beans before using them removes some of the salt, which is particularly helpful if you're watching your sodium intake.

Cilantro-Chili Sour Cream (below)

2 cans (15 ounces each) black beans, rinsed and drained

1 medium red bell pepper, chopped (1 cup)

2 medium green onions, chopped (2 tablespoons)

1 tablespoon chopped fresh parsley

1 tablespoon white wine vinegar

1 teaspoon grated lime or lemon peel

1/4 teaspoon red pepper sauce

Hot cooked rice, if desired

Make Cilantro-Chili Sour Cream. Mix remaining ingredients except rice in 2-quart saucepan. Cook about 2 minutes over medium-high heat, stirring occasionally, until hot. Serve with rice and sour cream.

Cilantro-Chili Sour Cream

1/2 cup fat-free sour cream

1 1/2 teaspoons chopped fresh cilantro

2 teaspoons olive or vegetable oil

2 teaspoons lime juice

1/4 teaspoon salt

1 jalapeño pepper, seeded and finely chopped (1 tablespoon)

Mix all ingredients until well blended.

NUTRITION INFORMATION
1 Serving

Calories 315 (Calories from Fat 35)
Fat 4g (Saturated 1g)
Cholesterol 0mg
Sodium 850mg
Carbohydrate 63g (Dietary Fiber 15g)
Protein 21g

% DAILY VALUE: Vitamin A 38%; Vitamin C 80%; Calcium 22%; Iron 32%

DIET EXCHANGES: 3 Starch, 3 Vegetable

greek salad toss

LOW FAT / LOW CHOLESTEROL

PREP: 15 min

4 SERVINGS

Stuff your pita pockets with a crunchy vegetable salad, or if you prefer, serve as a main-dish salad and keep the pitas on the side!

4 cups bite-size pieces salad greens

1 medium tomato, chopped (3/4 cup)

1 medium cucumber, chopped (1 cup)

1 medium onion, thinly sliced

1 can (15 to 16 ounces) garbanzo beans, rinsed and drained

1 can (14 ounces) artichoke hearts, drained and coarsely chopped

3/4 cup crumbled feta cheese (3 ounces)

1 tablespoon dried oregano leaves

2 cloves garlic, finely chopped

1/2 cup fat-free Caesar dressing

4 fat-free pita breads (6 inches in diameter), cut in half to form pockets

Mix all ingredients except dressing and pita breads in large bowl. Pour dressing over salad mixture; toss. Serve with pita bread halves.

NUTRITION INFORMATION
1 Serving

Calories 400 (Calories from Fat 70)
Fat 8g (Saturated 4g)
Cholesterol 20mg
Sodium 1050mg
Carbohydrate 74g (Dietary Fiber 12g)
Protein 20g

% DAILY VALUE: Vitamin A 8%; Vitamin C 26%; Calcium 24%; Iron 32%

DIET EXCHANGES: 4 Starch, 3 Vegetable, 1/2 Fat

BEANS HAVE BENEFITS

Beans are big on benefits. With more than twenty varieties to choose from, such as garbanzo, black, navy and kidney, beans are packed with nutrition and all sorts of health-promoting substances. Not only are they a protein powerhouse, they also are fat free and cholesterol free—two star qualities in terms of heart health.

And the news gets even better. Beans are rich in **folic acid, potassium** and **soluble fiber**—more heart helpers. Adding folic acid to a diet low in this vitamin may help lower homocysteine levels. High levels of homocysteine in the blood are linked to an increased risk for heart disease. Potassium helps keep blood pressure in check; high blood pressure is a risk factor for heart problems, too. Soluble fiber, which is also found in oats and some fruits and vegetables, has been shown to lower blood cholesterol when part of a low-fat diet.

Adding beans to your favorite dishes is quick and easy, especially when you use the canned varieties. Canned beans can be high in salt, so rinse them well if you are watching your sodium intake. You can also cook dried beans from scratch, which will require some planning ahead in terms of the time needed.

pesto-pepper pizza

LOW FAT / LOW CHOLESTEROL / LOW CALORIE

PREP: 15 min **BAKE:** 15 min
8 SERVINGS

Keeping pesto on hand can be a real lifesaver! Toss it with hot cooked pasta or steamed veggies for a delicious low-fat meal, or spread it on toasted bagels for a quick and easy snack.

Basil-Spinach Pesto (below)

1 package (10 ounces) ready-to-serve thin pizza crust (12 to 14 inches in diameter)

2 cups reduced-fat spaghetti sauce

1 medium green bell pepper, cut into rings

1 medium red bell pepper, cut into rings

1 cup shredded low-fat mozzarella cheese (4 ounces)

Heat oven to 500°. Make Basil-Spinach Pesto.

Place pizza crust on ungreased cookie sheet. Spread Basil-Spinach Pesto over crust. Top with spaghetti sauce and bell peppers. Sprinkle with cheese. Bake 10 to 15 minutes or until cheese is brown and bubbly.

Basil-Spinach Pesto

1/3 cup plain fat-free yogurt

1/3 cup soft bread crumbs

3 tablespoons grated reduced-fat or fat-free Parmesan cheese topping

1 tablespoon olive or vegetable oil

2 cloves garlic, finely chopped

2 cups lightly packed fresh basil leaves

1 cup chopped spinach leaves

Place all ingredients in food processor in order listed. Cover and process about 2 minutes, stopping occasionally to scrape side of bowl, until mixture is a thick paste.

NUTRITION INFORMATION
1 Serving

Calories 225 (Calories from Fat 65)
Fat 7g (Saturated 2g)
Cholesterol 10mg
Sodium 560mg
Carbohydrate 35g (Dietary Fiber 3g)
Protein 9g

% DAILY VALUE: Vitamin A 20%; Vitamin C 40%; Calcium 18%; Iron 12%

DIET EXCHANGES: 2 Starch, 1 Vegetable, 1 Fat

three-pepper stir-fry

LOW FAT / LOW CHOLESTEROL / LOW CALORIE

PREP: 10 min **COOK:** 10 min
4 SERVINGS

Hunting for hoisin sauce? This flavorful mixture of soybeans, garlic, chili peppers and various spices can be found in Asian markets and many large supermarkets.

1 can (14 1/2 ounces) ready-to-serve fat-free chicken broth

1 tablespoon grated gingerroot

3 cloves garlic, finely chopped

2 medium red bell peppers, thinly sliced

2 medium yellow bell peppers, thinly sliced

1 medium orange or green bell pepper, thinly sliced

1 1/2 tablespoons hoisin sauce

Hot cooked couscous, if desired

Heat half of the broth to boiling in nonstick wok or 10-inch skillet over medium-high heat. Add gingerroot and garlic; stir-fry 1 minute.

Add bell peppers and remaining broth. Cook 5 to 8 minutes, stirring occasionally, until bell peppers are tender and most of liquid has evaporated. Stir in hoisin sauce. Serve over couscous.

NUTRITION INFORMATION
1 Serving

Calories 75 (Calories from Fat 10)
Fat 1g (Saturated 0g)
Cholesterol 0mg
Sodium 570mg
Carbohydrate 15g (Dietary Fiber 3g)
Protein 4g

% DAILY VALUE: Vitamin A 40%; Vitamin C 100%; Calcium 2%; Iron 6%

DIET EXCHANGES: 3 Starch

provolone eggplant with chunky tomato vinaigrette

LOW FAT / LOW CHOLESTEROL / LOW CALORIE

PREP: 15 min **COOK:** 11 min **BROIL:** 2 min
4 SERVINGS

Chunky Tomato Vinaigrette (below)

Olive oil–flavored cooking spray

1 small unpeeled eggplant (about 1 pound), cut into eight 3/4-inch slices

1 1/2 teaspoons chopped fresh or 1/2 teaspoon dried basil leaves

1/4 teaspoon salt

2 ounces provolone or mozzarella cheese, cut into thin strips

Make Chunky Tomato Vinaigrette. Set oven control to broil. Spray 12-inch nonstick skillet with ovenproof handle with cooking spray; heat over medium heat. Spray both sides of eggplant slices with cooking spray. Place eggplant in skillet.

Sprinkle 3/4 teaspoon of the basil and 1/8 teaspoon of the salt evenly over eggplant slices. Cook 5 minutes; turn slices. Sprinkle with remaining 3/4 teaspoon basil and 1/8 teaspoon salt. Cook about 5 minutes or until tender; remove from heat.

Arrange cheese evenly on eggplant. Broil with tops about 3 inches from heat 1 to 2 minutes or until cheese is melted. Serve with vinaigrette.

Chunky Tomato Vinaigrette

2 large tomatoes, chopped (2 cups)

1 tablespoon chopped fresh or 1 teaspoon dried basil leaves

2 tablespoons capers

1 tablespoon red wine vinegar

1 tablespoon lemon juice

2 teaspoons olive or vegetable oil

1/2 teaspoon salt

2 cloves garlic, finely chopped

Mix all ingredients in glass or plastic bowl.

NUTRITION INFORMATION
1 Serving

Calories 120 (Calories from Fat 65)
Fat 7g (Saturated 3g)
Cholesterol 15mg
Sodium 260mg
Carbohydrate 13g (Dietary Fiber 4g)
Protein 5g

% DAILY VALUE: Vitamin A 10%; Vitamin C 16%; Calcium 12%; Iron 4%

DIET EXCHANGES: 3 Vegetable, 1 Fat

Provolone Eggplant with Chunky Tomato Vinaigrette

smashed potato soup

LOW FAT / LOW CHOLESTEROL / LOW CALORIE

PREP: 10 min **COOK:** 25 min
6 SERVINGS

This soup is so thick and creamy, you'll want to make it the star of your meal. Partner it with a loaf of crusty French bread and a fresh garden salad for a stick-to-your-ribs dinner.

3 1/2 cups fat-free (skim) milk

3 tablespoons all-purpose flour

2 teaspoons margarine

1 large onion, finely chopped (1 cup)

4 medium unpeeled potatoes (1 1/2 pounds), cut into 1/4-inch pieces

1 1/2 teaspoons salt

1/4 teaspoon black pepper

1/8 teaspoon ground red pepper (cayenne)

1 1/4 cups shredded reduced-fat sharp Cheddar cheese (5 ounces)

1/3 cup fat-free sour cream

8 medium green onions, sliced (1/2 cup)

Beat 1/2 cup of the milk and the flour with wire whisk until smooth; set aside.

Melt margarine in 4-quart Dutch oven over medium heat. Cook onion in margarine about 3 minutes, stirring occasionally, until tender. Increase heat to high; stir in remaining 3 cups milk. Stir in potatoes, salt, black pepper and red pepper. Heat to boiling; reduce heat to low. Simmer uncovered 15 to 18 minutes, stirring frequently, until potatoes are tender.

Beat in flour mixture with wire whisk. Cook about 2 minutes, stirring frequently, until thickened; remove from heat.

Beat potato mixture with wire whisk until potatoes are slightly mashed. Stir in cheese, sour cream and green onions.

NUTRITION INFORMATION
1 Serving

Calories 210 (Calories from Fat 25)
Fat 3g (Saturated 1g)
Cholesterol 10mg
Sodium 840mg
Carbohydrate 35g (Dietary Fiber 3g)
Protein 14g

% DAILY VALUE: Vitamin A 14%; Vitamin C 12%; Calcium 32%; Iron 8%

DIET EXCHANGES: 1 Starch, 1 Vegetable, 1 Skim Milk

LOW-FAT COOKING 101: CREAMY SOUPS *WITHOUT* CREAM

You don't have to give up the rich, hearty texture of a thick cream soup—just the guilt. For wonderfully creamy low-fat soup, try one of these simple soup thickeners:

Mix in some mashed potatoes or cooked rice.
Place potatoes or rice with a little of the soup liquid in a blender. Cover and blend until smooth. Stir into soup.

Make a purée.
Puree one or more of the vegetables used in a soup or stew by placing the cooked vegetable in a blender or food processor with a little of the soup liquid. Cover and blend until smooth. Stir the mixture into the soup. Or blend all of the soup with some fat-free (skim) milk, fat-free sour cream or plain fat-free yogurt.

Add dry instant mashed potato mix.
Stir in 1 tablespoon at a time, and cook for 1 minute. Soup still too thin? Add a little more. Be careful not to add it too quickly, however, as it is easier to put it in than it is to take it out.

low fat

Main-dish recipes have 10 or fewer grams of fat per serving.
Low-fat side dishes and desserts have 3 or fewer grams of fat per serving.

low cholesterol

Recipes have 90 or fewer milligrams of cholesterol per serving.

low calorie

Recipes have 350 or fewer calories per serving with the exception of desserts.
Low-calorie desserts have 250 or fewer calories per serving.

CHAPTER 5

salads & sides

Sherried Greens with Fruit & Blue Cheese (page 159)

bacon-spinach salad

LOW FAT / LOW CHOLESTEROL / LOW CALORIE

PREP: 5 min **COOK:** 10 min
4 SERVINGS

For a touch of sweetness and color, use raspberry vinegar in place of the white vinegar and sprinkle the salad with fresh raspberries.

4 slices bacon, diced

1/4 cup white vinegar

4 teaspoons sugar

1/4 teaspoon salt

1/8 teaspoon pepper

1 bag (10 ounces) washed fresh spinach

5 medium green onions, chopped (1/3 cup)

Cook bacon in 12-inch skillet over medium heat, stirring occasionally, until crisp. Stir in vinegar, sugar, salt and pepper. Heat through, stirring constantly, until sugar is dissolved; remove from heat.

Add spinach and onions to bacon mixture. Toss 1 to 2 minutes or until spinach is wilted.

NUTRITION INFORMATION
1 Serving

Calories 65 (Calories from Fat 25)
Fat 3g (Saturated 1g)
Cholesterol 5mg
Sodium 280mg
Carbohydrate 8g (Dietary Fiber 2g)
Protein 3g

% DAILY VALUE: Vitamin A 34%; Vitamin C 24%; Calcium 6%; Iron 8%

DIET EXCHANGES: 2 Vegetable, 1/2 Fat

sherried greens with fruit & blue cheese

LOW FAT / LOW CHOLESTEROL / LOW CALORIE

PREP: 15 min
8 SERVINGS

Toasted sesame oil is what gives this salad its distinctively nutty flavor. If you can't find sesame oil, you can substitute vegetable oil and sprinkle the salad with toasted sesame seed.

1/4 cup dry sherry or apple juice

2 tablespoons balsamic or red wine vinegar

1 tablespoon sugar

1 teaspoon toasted sesame oil

8 cups bite-size pieces mixed salad greens

1 medium pear, thinly sliced

1 cup sliced strawberries

1 small red onion, thinly sliced

1/4 cup finely crumbled blue cheese (1 ounce)

Mix sherry, vinegar, sugar and oil until sugar is dissolved.

Arrange salad greens, pear, strawberries and onion on 8 salad plates. Pour sherry mixture over salads. Sprinkle with cheese.

NUTRITION INFORMATION
1 Serving

Calories 55 (Calories from Fat 20)
Fat 2g (Saturated 1g)
Cholesterol 5mg
Sodium 55mg
Carbohydrate 9g (Dietary Fiber 2g)
Protein 2g

% DAILY VALUE: Vitamin A 6%; Vitamin C 30%; Calcium 4%; Iron 2%

DIET EXCHANGES: 2 Vegetable

couscous salad with artichokes & red peppers

LOW CHOLESTEROL / LOW CALORIE

PREP: 15 min **COOK:** 5 min **STAND:** 15 min
6 SERVINGS

1 cup water

3/4 cup uncooked couscous

6 roma (plum) tomatoes, chopped (2 cups)

1 can (14 ounces) artichoke heart quarters, drained and chopped

1 jar (7 ounces) roasted red bell peppers, drained and cut into thin strips

1 can (2 1/4 ounces) sliced ripe olives, drained

1/2 cup finely chopped fresh parsley

1/4 cup finely chopped red onion

3 tablespoons cider vinegar

1/2 teaspoon salt

2 cloves garlic, finely chopped

1/3 cup crumbled feta cheese (1 1/2 ounces)

Heat water to boiling in 10-inch nonstick skillet. Stir in couscous; remove from heat. Cover and let stand about 5 minutes or until water is absorbed.

Fluff couscous with fork. Spread couscous evenly in thin layer on cookie sheet. Let stand 8 to 10 minutes or until cool.

Mix remaining ingredients except cheese in medium bowl. Add couscous and cheese to tomato mixture. Gently toss until mixed.

NUTRITION INFORMATION
1 Serving

Calories 170 (Calories from Fat 35)
Fat 4g (Saturated 2g)
Cholesterol 5mg
Sodium 400mg
Carbohydrate 31g (Dietary Fiber 6g)
Protein 8g

% DAILY VALUE: Vitamin A 18%; Vitamin C 100%; Calcium 10%; Iron 12%

DIET EXCHANGES: 1 Starch, 3 Vegetable, 1/2 Fat

tangy coleslaw

LOW FAT / LOW CHOLESTEROL / LOW CALORIE

PREP: 15 min **CHILL:** 2 hr
6 SERVINGS

Tangy Dressing (below)

4 cups finely chopped cabbage (1 pound)

1/2 cup chopped peeled jicama

1 small green bell pepper, chopped (1/2 cup)

1 small carrot, shredded (1/2 cup)

1 medium onion, diced (1/2 cup)

6 medium radishes, sliced (1/2 cup)

Make Tangy Dressing. Toss dressing and remaining ingredients. Cover and refrigerate about 2 hours or until chilled.

Tangy Dressing

3 tablespoons packed brown sugar

3 tablespoons water

3 tablespoons red wine vinegar

1 tablespoon vegetable oil

1/4 teaspoon salt

1 clove garlic, finely chopped

Mix all ingredients.

NUTRITION INFORMATION
1 Serving

Calories 75 (Calories from Fat 25)
Fat 3g (Saturated 0g)
Cholesterol 0mg
Sodium 115mg
Carbohydrate 14g (Dietary Fiber 3g)
Protein 1g

% DAILY VALUE: Vitamin A 16%; Vitamin C 58%; Calcium 4%; Iron 4%

DIET EXCHANGES: 3 Vegetable

wild rice salad with dried cherries

LOW FAT / LOW CHOLESTEROL / LOW CALORIE

PREP: 20 min **COOK:** 20 min
8 SERVINGS

Transform this side-dish salad into a main-meal masterpiece. Add 2 cups chopped cooked chicken or turkey breast and 1/2 cup chopped dried apricots. Turn up the heat by sprinkling in 1/4 teaspoon crushed red pepper.

1 package (6 1/4 ounces) fast-cooking long-grain and wild rice mix

1 medium unpeeled eating apple, chopped (1 cup)

1 medium green bell pepper, chopped (1 cup)

1 medium stalk celery, chopped (1/2 cup)

2/3 cup dried cherries, chopped

2 tablespoons reduced-sodium soy sauce

2 tablespoons water

2 teaspoons sugar

2 teaspoons cider vinegar

1/3 cup dry-roasted peanuts, toasted (page 82)

Cook rice mix as directed on package—except omit margarine. Spread rice evenly in thin layer on large cookie sheet. Let stand 10 to 12 minutes, stirring occasionally, until cool.

Mix apple, bell pepper, celery and cherries in large bowl. Mix soy sauce, water, sugar and vinegar in small bowl until sugar is dissolved. Add rice and soy sauce mixture to apple mixture. Gently toss until coated. Add peanuts; gently toss.

NUTRITION INFORMATION
1 Serving

Calories 110 (Calories from Fat 25)
Fat 3g (Saturated 0g)
Cholesterol 0mg
Sodium 170mg
Carbohydrate 23g (Dietary Fiber 5g)
Protein 3g

% DAILY VALUE: Vitamin A 0%; Vitamin C 22%; Calcium 2%; Iron 4%

DIET EXCHANGES: 1 Starch, 1/2 Fruit

NEWS ABOUT NUTS AND CHOLESTEROL

Peanuts, walnuts and other nuts used to be taboo foods for the health conscious, primarily because they are high in fat. This attitude may be changing as more new research shows that nuts have something good to offer.

Peanuts contain resveratrol, the same compound in red wine that scientists believe may lower blood cholesterol levels. Peanuts are also rich in monounsaturated fat, vitamin E and folic acid, all heart-healthy nutrients.

Walnuts are grabbing headlines because they, too, may help lower blood cholesterol levels. A fatty acid in walnuts called alpha-linolenic is believed to reduce the risk for blood clot formation and artery clogging. (Alpha-linolenic acid is related to the omega-3 fatty acids found in fish.) One study found that people who consumed walnut oil had higher HDL levels than those who never ate walnuts or used the oil.

Though nuts have their benefits, they still are considered a higher-fat food, so limit yourself to just a few and eat them only occasionally.

Wild Rice Salad with Dried Cherries

festive broccoli & corn

LOW FAT / LOW CHOLESTEROL / LOW CALORIE

PREP: 10 min **COOK:** 8 min
4 SERVINGS

1 package (10 ounces) frozen broccoli cuts
or broccoli flowerets

1 cup frozen whole kernel corn

1 jar (2 ounces) diced pimientos, drained

1 medium onion, chopped (1/2 cup)

1/2 cup water

2 teaspoons chopped fresh or 1/2 teaspoon
dried basil leaves

1/2 teaspoon chicken bouillon granules

1 clove garlic, finely chopped

Heat all ingredients to boiling in 1 1/2-quart saucepan; reduce heat to low.
Cover and simmer 4 to 5 minutes or until broccoli is crisp-tender.

NUTRITION INFORMATION
1 Serving

Calories 60 (Calories from Fat 0)
Fat 0g (Saturated 0g)
Cholesterol 0mg
Sodium 180mg
Carbohydrate 15g (Dietary Fiber 4g)
Protein 4g

% DAILY VALUE: Vitamin A 16%; Vitamin C
34%; Calcium 4%; Iron 4%

DIET EXCHANGES: 3 Vegetable

Festive Broccoli & Corn

harvest roasted vegetables

LOW FAT / LOW CHOLESTEROL / LOW CALORIE

PREP: 10 min **BROIL:** 12 min
4 SERVINGS

Forget the notion that roasted vegetables take a long time to cook. This quick-to-fix veggie sidekick is ideal for hectic schedules. Serve alongside grilled fish or chicken, or top off baked potatoes or a bowl of pasta for a virtually effortless meal.

1 medium green bell pepper, cut into 1-inch pieces

1 medium onion, cut into 1/4-inch wedges

1 medium tomato, cut into 1/4-inch wedges

1 medium zucchini, cut into 1-inch pieces

Olive oil–flavored cooking spray

1/2 teaspoon salt

Set oven control to broil. Cover cookie sheet with aluminum foil; spray with cooking spray. Place vegetables in single layer on cookie sheet. Spray vegetables with cooking spray. Sprinkle with 1/4 teaspoon of the salt.

Broil with tops 4 inches from heat about 12 minutes, stirring occasionally, until vegetables are tender. Sprinkle with remaining 1/4 teaspoon salt.

NUTRITION INFORMATION
1 Serving

Calories 25 (Calories from Fat 0)
Fat 0g (Saturated 0g)
Cholesterol 0mg
Sodium 300mg
Carbohydrate 7g (Dietary Fiber 2g)
Protein 1g

% DAILY VALUE: Vitamin A 4%; Vitamin C 32%; Calcium 2%; Iron 2%

DIET EXCHANGES: 1 Vegetable

sweet potato surprise

LOW FAT / LOW CHOLESTEROL / LOW CALORIE

PREP: 15 min **BAKE:** 10 min
6 SERVINGS

The surprise in this side dish is the marshmallow hidden inside a ball of mashed sweet potato! To top it off, the balls are brushed with melted margarine and rolled in cornflake crumbs for a buttery, crisp coating.

1 can (18 ounces) vacuum-pack sweet potatoes

1 tablespoon packed brown sugar

6 large marshmallows

1 tablespoon margarine, melted

1/3 cup cornflake crumbs

Heat oven to 450°. Grease square pan, 8 × 8 × 2 inches. Mash sweet potatoes and brown sugar. Shape 1/3 cup potato mixture around each marshmallow into a ball.

Brush 1 sweet potato ball at a time with margarine; roll in cornflake crumbs to coat. Place in pan. Bake uncovered 8 to 10 minutes or until coating is light brown.

NUTRITION INFORMATION
1 Serving

Calories 125 (Calories from Fat 20)
Fat 2g (Saturated 0g)
Cholesterol 0mg
Sodium 90mg
Carbohydrate 27g (Dietary Fiber 2g)
Protein 2g

% DAILY VALUE: Vitamin A 70%; Vitamin C 18%; Calcium 2%; Iron 6%

DIET EXCHANGES: 1 Starch, 1 Fruit

horseradish mashed potatoes

LOW FAT / LOW CHOLESTEROL / LOW CALORIE

PREP: 10 min **COOK:** 20 min
4 SERVINGS

If you prefer a milder flavor, use horseradish sauce in place of the prepared horseradish and decrease the yogurt to 1/4 cup. Horseradish sauce looks like mayonnaise and is higher in calories and fat than prepared horseradish. You can find it next to the bottled tartar sauce and mayonnaise in your supermarket.

4 medium unpeeled boiling potatoes (about 1 1/2 pounds), cut into 1/2-inch slices

1/3 cup plain fat-free yogurt

1 tablespoon prepared horseradish

1/2 teaspoon salt

2 to 4 tablespoons fat-free (skim) milk

Chopped fresh parsley, if desired

Heat 1 inch water to boiling in 3-quart saucepan. Add potatoes. Heat to boiling; reduce heat to low. Simmer uncovered about 15 minutes or until tender; drain. Return potatoes to saucepan. Shake pan with potatoes over low heat to dry; remove from heat.

Mash potatoes until no lumps remain. Beat in yogurt, horseradish and salt. Add milk in small amounts, beating after each addition (amount of milk needed to make potatoes smooth and fluffy depends on the kind of potatoes used). Beat vigorously until potatoes are light and fluffy. Sprinkle with parsley.

NUTRITION INFORMATION
1 Serving

Calories 135 (Calories from Fat 0)
Fat 0g (Saturated 0g)
Cholesterol 0mg
Sodium 330mg
Carbohydrate 33g (Dietary Fiber 3g)
Protein 4g

% DAILY VALUE: Vitamin A 0%; Vitamin C 14%; Calcium 6%; Iron 10%

DIET EXCHANGES: 2 Starch

Horseradish Mashed Potatoes

low fat

Main-dish recipes have 10 or fewer grams of fat per serving.
Low-fat side dishes and desserts have 3 or fewer grams of fat per serving.

low cholesterol

Recipes have 90 or fewer milligrams of cholesterol per serving.

low calorie

Recipes have 350 or fewer calories per serving with the exception of desserts.
Low-calorie desserts have 250 or fewer calories per serving.

CHAPTER 6

breads & breakfast dishes

Cranberry Pancakes with Maple-Orange Syrup (page 188)

buttermilk corn bread

LOW FAT / LOW CHOLESTEROL / LOW CALORIE

PREP: 15 min **BAKE:** 30 min

12 SERVINGS

Buttermilk is a low-fat baker's bargain! Despite its name, buttermilk has only 100 calories and 2.5 grams of fat per cup. If you don't have buttermilk on hand, use 1 1/2 tablespoons lemon juice or vinegar plus enough skim milk to equal 1 1/2 cups. Let the mixture stand about 10 minutes or until slightly thickened.

1 1/2 cups yellow cornmeal

1/2 cup all-purpose flour

1 1/2 cups buttermilk

2 tablespoons vegetable oil

2 teaspoons baking powder

1 teaspoon sugar

1 teaspoon salt

1/2 teaspoon baking soda

1/2 cup fat-free cholesterol-free egg product or 4 egg whites

Heat oven to 450°. Grease bottom and side of round pan, 9 × 1 1/2 inches, or square pan, 8 × 8 × 2 inches.

Mix all ingredients. Beat vigorously 30 seconds. Pour batter into pan. Bake 25 to 30 minutes or until golden brown. Serve warm.

NUTRITION INFORMATION
1 Serving

Calories 110 (Calories from Fat 25)
Fat 3g (Saturated 1g)
Cholesterol 5mg
Sodium 370mg
Carbohydrate 19g (Dietary Fiber 2g)
Protein 4g

% DAILY VALUE: Vitamin A 2%; Vitamin C 0%; Calcium 8%; Iron 6%

DIET EXCHANGES: 1 1/2 Starch

ginger-topped pumpkin bread

LOW FAT / LOW CHOLESTEROL / LOW CALORIE

PREP: 15 min **BAKE:** 1 hr 10 min **COOL:** 1 hr
2 LOAVES (24 slices each)

1 can (15 ounces) pumpkin

1 2/3 cups sugar

2/3 cup unsweetened applesauce

1/2 cup milk

2 teaspoons vanilla

1 cup fat-free cholesterol-free egg product
or 2 eggs plus 4 egg whites

3 cups all-purpose flour

2 teaspoons baking soda

1 teaspoon salt

1 teaspoon ground cinnamon

1/2 teaspoon baking powder

1/2 teaspoon ground cloves

Vanilla Glaze (right)

3 tablespoons finely chopped crystallized
ginger, if desired

Move oven rack to low position so that tops of pans will be in center of oven. Heat oven to 350°. Grease bottoms only of 2 loaf pans, 8 1/2 × 4 1/2 × 2 1/2 or 9 × 5 × 3 inches.

Mix pumpkin, sugar, applesauce, milk, vanilla and egg product in large bowl. Stir in remaining ingredients except Vanilla Glaze and ginger. Pour into pans.

Bake 60 to 70 minutes or until toothpick inserted in center comes out clean. Cool 10 minutes. Loosen sides of loaves from pans; remove from pans to wire rack. Cool completely, about 1 hour. Drizzle with Vanilla Glaze. Sprinkle with ginger.

Vanilla Glaze

2/3 cup powdered sugar

2 to 3 teaspoons warm water

1/4 teaspoon vanilla

Mix all ingredients until smooth and thin enough to drizzle.

raspberry crumble muffins

LOW FAT / LOW CHOLESTEROL / LOW CALORIE

PREP: 15 min **BAKE:** 25 min
12 MUFFINS

1/4 cup firmly packed brown sugar

1/2 teaspoon ground cinnamon

1 cup fat-free (skim) milk

1/4 cup unsweetened applesauce

2 tablespoons vegetable oil

1/2 teaspoon vanilla

1/4 cup fat-free cholesterol-free egg product or 2 egg whites

2 cups all-purpose flour

1/3 cup granulated sugar

3 teaspoons baking powder

1/2 teaspoon salt

1 cup fresh or frozen (thawed and drained) raspberries

Heat oven to 400°. Grease bottoms only of 12 medium muffin cups, 2 1/2 × 1 1/4 inches, or line with paper baking cups. Mix brown sugar and cinnamon; set aside.

Beat milk, applesauce, oil, vanilla and egg product in large bowl. Stir in flour, granulated sugar, baking powder and salt all at once just until flour is moistened (batter will be lumpy). Fold in raspberries. Divide batter evenly among muffin cups. Sprinkle brown sugar mixture evenly over tops of muffins.

Bake 20 to 25 minutes or until golden brown. Immediately remove from pan to wire rack. Serve warm if desired.

NUTRITION INFORMATION
1 Muffin

Calories 155 (Calories from Fat 25)
Fat 3g (Saturated 0g)
Cholesterol 0mg
Sodium 240mg
Carbohydrate 30g (Dietary Fiber 1g)
Protein 3g

% DAILY VALUE: Vitamin A 2%; Vitamin C 2%; Calcium 10%; Iron 8%

DIET EXCHANGES: 1 Starch, 1 Fruit, 1/2 Fat

Raspberry Crumble Muffins and Tropical Smoothie (page 185)

lemon-berry brunch cake

LOW CHOLESTEROL / LOW CALORIE

PREP: 15 min **BAKE:** 45 min **COOL:** 10 min

10 SERVINGS

1 cup lemon low-fat yogurt

3 tablespoons vegetable oil

1/4 cup fat-free cholesterol-free egg product or 2 egg whites

1/2 cup sugar

2 cups all-purpose flour

1 tablespoon grated lemon peel

2 teaspoons baking powder

1/2 teaspoon baking soda

1/4 teaspoon salt

1 1/2 cups fresh or frozen (thawed and drained) blueberries

Lemon Glaze (above)

Heat oven to 375°. Spray square pan, 9 × 9 × 2 inches, with cooking spray.

Beat yogurt, oil, egg product and sugar in large bowl. Stir in remaining ingredients except blueberries and Lemon Glaze. Carefully stir in blueberries. Spread in pan.

Bake about 45 minutes or until cake springs back when touched lightly in center. Cool 10 minutes. Drizzle with Lemon Glaze. Serve warm or cool.

Lemon Glaze

2/3 cup powdered sugar

3 to 4 teaspoons lemon juice

Mix all ingredients until smooth.

NUTRITION INFORMATION
1 Serving

Calories 235 (Calories from Fat 45)
Fat 5g (Saturated 1g)
Cholesterol 0mg
Sodium 240mg
Carbohydrate 45g (Dietary Fiber 1g)
Protein 4g

% DAILY VALUE: Vitamin A 0%; Vitamin C 2%; Calcium 10%; Iron 8%

DIET EXCHANGES: 2 Starch, 1 Fruit, 1/2 Fat

BERRY GOOD NEWS

Researchers looked at forty different fruits, vegetables and juices to measure which were the most potent in their antioxidant capabilities. Guess what? Blueberries took home the blue ribbon.

Blueberries are packed with anthocyanins, powerful antioxidants usually found in deep red and purple foods. Antioxidants work by mopping up free radicals, the damaged and unstable molecules created when your body converts food to energy. Free radicals travel through the body damaging cells, and that damage may contribute to or accelerate the risk for cancer and heart disease. Some antioxidants block the attack of free radicals on cells; other antioxidants neutralize free radicals and convert them into safe substances.

Beyond blueberries, some other anthocyanin sources include red cabbage, grapes, strawberries, plums and cherries.

Lemon-Berry Brunch Cake

apricot-oat scones

LOW CHOLESTEROL / LOW CALORIE

PREP: 15 min **BAKE:** 18 min
12 SCONES

Oats, a good source of soluble fiber (beta glucan), act as little sponges that soak up cholesterol and take it out of the body.

1 cup all-purpose flour

1/4 cup packed brown sugar

1 1/2 teaspoons baking powder

1/4 teaspoon baking soda

1/4 teaspoon salt

3 tablespoons firm margarine

1/2 cup quick-cooking or old-fashioned oats

1/2 cup oat bran

1/2 cup chopped dried apricots

1/4 cup fat-free cholesterol-free egg product or 2 egg whites

About 1/2 cup buttermilk

Heat oven to 400°. Mix flour, brown sugar, baking powder, baking soda and salt in large bowl. Cut in margarine, using pastry blender or criss-crossing 2 knives, until mixture looks like fine crumbs. Stir in oats, oat bran and apricots. Stir in egg product and just enough buttermilk so dough leaves side of bowl and forms a ball.

Turn dough onto lightly floured surface; gently roll in flour to coat. Knead lightly 10 times. Place on ungreased cookie sheet; pat into 8-inch circle, using floured hands. Cut into 12 wedges with sharp knife dipped in flour, but do not separate wedges. Brush with additional buttermilk and sprinkle with oats if desired.

Bake 16 to 18 minutes or until golden brown. Remove from cookie sheet; separate wedges. Serve warm.

NUTRITION INFORMATION
1 Scone

Calories 125 (Calories from Fat 35)
Fat 4g (Saturated 1g)
Cholesterol 0mg
Sodium 150mg
Carbohydrate 21g (Dietary Fiber 2g)
Protein 3g

% DAILY VALUE: Vitamin A 8%; Vitamin C 0%; Calcium 6%; Iron 6%

DIET EXCHANGES: 1 Starch, 1/2 Fruit, 1/2 Fat

fruit-topped breakfast bagels

LOW FAT / LOW CHOLESTEROL / LOW CALORIE

PREP: 10 min
4 SERVINGS

If you can't find premixed cinnamon and sugar in your supermarket (sold in the spice or sugar section), simply mix together granulated sugar and desired amount of ground cinnamon in a small plastic container with a lid.

1/3 cup diced banana

1/3 cup chopped fresh or canned (drained) peaches

1/3 cup fresh raspberries

1/4 cup orange or vanilla low-fat yogurt

2 bagels, split in half

1 tablespoon prepared cinnamon-sugar

Mix banana, peaches, raspberries and yogurt.

Toast bagels. Sprinkle cinnamon-sugar evenly over warm bagel halves. Top each bagel half with 1/4 cup fruit mixture.

mocha mudslide cooler

LOW FAT / LOW CHOLESTEROL / LOW CALORIE

PREP: 10 min
2 SERVINGS

Banana is what gives this breakfast shake its thick and creamy appeal! To make sure you always have bananas on hand, peel them and freeze in plastic wrap. Just use a little less ice when whipping up this drink with frozen bananas.

1 medium banana, cut into chunks

1 cup fat-free (skim) milk

1 tablespoon sugar

2 teaspoons baking cocoa

1 teaspoon powdered instant coffee (dry)

1/2 teaspoon vanilla

3 or 4 ice cubes

Place all ingredients except ice cubes in blender. Cover and blend on high speed about 15 seconds or until smooth. Add ice cubes. Cover and blend about 15 seconds or until blended. Serve immediately.

NUTRITION INFORMATION
1 Serving

Calories 130 (Calories from Fat 10)
Fat 1g (Saturated 0g)
Cholesterol 5mg
Sodium 65mg
Carbohydrate 27g (Dietary Fiber 2g)
Protein 5g

% DAILY VALUE: Vitamin A 8%; Vitamin C 10%; Calcium 16%; Iron 2%

DIET EXCHANGES: 1 Fruit, 1 Skim Milk

tropical smoothie

LOW FAT / LOW CHOLESTEROL / LOW CALORIE

PREP: 5 min
4 SERVINGS

Besides being low in fat, this simple sipper is a calcium powerhouse. To triple the calcium hit, use calcium-fortified orange juice instead of the pineapple juice.

1 cup vanilla low-fat yogurt

1 cup cut-up mango or peach

1/3 cup fat-free (skim) milk

1/4 cup pineapple juice

Place all ingredients in blender. Cover and blend on medium speed about 45 seconds or until thick and smooth. Serve immediately.

NUTRITION INFORMATION
1 Serving

Calories 110 (Calories from Fat 10)
Fat 1g (Saturated 0g)
Cholesterol 5mg
Sodium 45mg
Carbohydrate 22g (Dietary Fiber 1g)
Protein 4g

% DAILY VALUE: Vitamin A 18%; Vitamin C 22%; Calcium 12%; Iron 0%

DIET EXCHANGES: 1 Fruit, 1/2 Skim Milk

stuffed french toast

LOW FAT / LOW CHOLESTEROL / LOW CALORIE

PREP: 15 min **COOK:** 6 min
6 SERVINGS

12 slices French bread, 1/2 inch thick

6 tablespoons fat-free soft cream cheese

1/4 cup preserves or jam (any flavor)

1/2 cup fat-free cholesterol-free egg product
or 4 egg whites, slightly beaten

1/2 cup fat-free (skim) milk

2 tablespoons granulated sugar

Powdered sugar

Maple-flavored syrup, if desired

Spread one side of 6 slices bread with 1 tablespoon of the cream cheese. Spread one side of remaining slices with 2 teaspoons of the preserves. Place bread with cream cheese and bread with preserves together in pairs.

Beat egg product, milk and granulated sugar until smooth; pour into shallow bowl.

Spray griddle or skillet with cooking spray; heat griddle or skillet over medium-low heat or to 325°. Dip each side of sandwich into egg mixture. Cook sandwiches 2 to 3 minutes on each side or until golden brown. Transfer to plate; dust with powdered sugar. Serve with syrup.

NUTRITION INFORMATION
1 Serving

Calories 205 (Calories from Fat 20)
Fat 2g (Saturated 0g)
Cholesterol 0mg
Sodium 410mg
Carbohydrate 40g (Dietary Fiber 2g)
Protein 9g

% DAILY VALUE: Vitamin A 10%; Vitamin C 0%; Calcium 12%; Iron 10%

DIET EXCHANGES: 2 Starch, 1/2 Skim Milk

Stuffed French Toast

home-style scrambled eggs

LOW FAT / LOW CHOLESTEROL / LOW CALORIE

PREP: 10 min **COOK:** 10 min
4 SERVINGS

Do your scrambled eggs end up looking more like rice or peas than the eggs served at a restaurant? The trick is to avoid stirring them as much as possible while they cook.

1 1/2 cups fat-free cholesterol-free egg product

3/4 teaspoon salt

3 tablespoons water

1 tablespoon margarine

1 cup refrigerated diced potatoes with onions or frozen hash brown potatoes

1 small zucchini, chopped (1 cup)

1 medium tomato, seeded and chopped (3/4 cup)

Mix egg product, salt and water; set aside.

Spray 10-inch nonstick skillet with cooking spray. Melt margarine in skillet over medium heat. Cook potatoes, zucchini and tomato in margarine, stirring occasionally, until hot.

Pour egg product mixture over vegetable mixture. As egg mixture begins to set at bottom and side, gently lift cooked portions with spatula so that thin, uncooked portion can flow to bottom. Avoid constant stirring. Cook 3 to 4 minutes or until eggs are thickened throughout but still moist.

NUTRITION INFORMATION
1 Serving

Calories 110 (Calories from Fat 25)
Fat 3g (Saturated 1g)
Cholesterol 0mg
Sodium 620mg
Carbohydrate 14g (Dietary Fiber 2g)
Protein 9g

% DAILY VALUE: Vitamin A 10%; Vitamin C 10%; Calcium 4%; Iron 12%

DIET EXCHANGES: 1 Starch, 1 Very Lean Meat

Home-Style Scrambled Eggs

hash brown frittata

LOW FAT / LOW CHOLESTEROL / LOW CALORIE

PREP: 10 min **COOK:** 25 min
4 SERVINGS

Add some kick to this frittata by topping it off with your favorite salsa or barbecue sauce. Serve each wedge with a spoonful of barbecue sauce or 1/2 cup of salsa on the side.

2 cups refrigerated shredded hash brown potatoes (from 1-pound 4-ounce bag)

1 can (11 ounces) whole kernel corn with red and green peppers, drained

1 teaspoon onion salt

1 cup fat-free cholesterol-free egg product

1/4 cup fat-free (skim) milk

1/2 teaspoon dried marjoram leaves

1/2 teaspoon red pepper sauce

1/3 cup shredded reduced-fat Cheddar cheese

Mix potatoes, corn and onion salt. Spray 10-inch nonstick skillet with cooking spray; heat over medium heat. Pack potato mixture firmly into skillet, leaving 1/2-inch space around edge. Reduce heat to medium-low. Cook uncovered about 10 minutes or until bottom starts to brown.

While potato mixture is cooking, mix egg product, milk, marjoram and pepper sauce. Pour egg mixture over potato mixture. Cook uncovered over medium-low heat. As egg mixture begins to set on bottom and side, gently lift cooked portions with spatula so that thin, uncooked portion can flow to bottom. Avoid constant stirring. Cook about 5 minutes or until eggs are thickened throughout but still moist.

Sprinkle with cheese. Reduce heat to low. Cover and cook about 10 minutes or until center is set and cheese is bubbly. Loosen bottom of frittata with spatula. Cut frittata into 4 wedges. Serve immediately.

NUTRITION INFORMATION
1 Serving

Calories 220 (Calories from Fat 20)
Fat 2g (Saturated 1g)
Cholesterol 5mg
Sodium 720mg
Carbohydrate 43g (Dietary Fiber 5g)
Protein 12g

% DAILY VALUE: Vitamin A 6%; Vitamin C 18%; Calcium 10%; Iron 12%

DIET EXCHANGES: 3 Starch

wild rice frittata

LOW FAT / LOW CHOLESTEROL / LOW CALORIE

PREP: 10 min **COOK:** 25 min **STAND:** 5 min
6 SERVINGS

1 tablespoon margarine

1 large bell pepper, chopped (1 cup)

1 medium onion, chopped (1/2 cup)

1 1/2 cups fat-free cholesterol-free egg product

1/4 cup fat-free (skim) milk

1 cup cooked wild rice

1 cup shredded reduced-fat Swiss cheese (4 ounces)

Melt margarine in 10-inch nonstick skillet over medium heat. Cook bell pepper and onion in margarine, stirring occasionally, until vegetables are crisp-tender.

Mix egg product, milk, wild rice and 1/2 cup of the cheese; pour over vegetables. Reduce heat to low. Cover and cook 15 to 20 minutes or until eggs are set; remove from heat. Sprinkle with remaining 1/2 cup cheese. Cover and let stand about 5 minutes or until cheese is melted. Cut into wedges. Serve immediately.

EGGS—YEA OR NAY?

First eggs were good for you, then they were not. Now it looks as though they are not so bad after all. Which is it?

Eggs have some excellent attributes, including being rich in protein, B vitamins and iron, all of which are good for your health. In short, eating some eggs is fine, but the American Heart Association recommends that people eat no more than three to four egg *yolks* per week.

If you are watching your cholesterol, you may need to be a little more conservative in the number of eggs you eat, particularly the yolks. Egg yolks are high in cholesterol (about 215 milligrams); for some people, eating too much cholesterol may increase the amount of cholesterol circulating in the blood. One healthy option is to use the eggs, but leave out the yolks. Leaving out the yolks is easy to do, especially when you get creative in cooking. You can often substitute two egg whites for one whole egg or use fat-free cholesterol-free egg product.

While you're watching the cholesterol, be sure to watch the fat, too. Although one egg contains less than 5 grams of fat, eggs are often partnered with fairly high-fat foods, such as bacon, sausage and baked goods. They're also often cooked in butter or coupled with high-fat sauces like hollandaise.

NUTRITION INFORMATION
1 Serving

Calories 135 (Calories from Fat 45)
Fat 5g (Saturated 2g)
Cholesterol 10mg
Sodium 160mg
Carbohydrate 11g (Dietary Fiber 2g)
Protein 13g

% DAILY VALUE: Vitamin A 100%; Vitamin C 12%; Calcium 100%; Iron 0%

DIET EXCHANGES: 1 Starch, 1 1/2 Very Lean Meat

low fat

Main-dish recipes have 10 or fewer grams of fat per serving.

Low-fat side dishes and desserts have 3 or fewer grams of fat per serving.

low cholesterol

Recipes have 90 or fewer milligrams of cholesterol per serving.

low calorie

Recipes have 350 or fewer calories per serving with the exception of desserts.

Low-calorie desserts have 250 or fewer calories per serving.

desserts & sweet treats

Chocolate-Cherry Sundae Cake (page 196)

chocolate-cherry sundae cake

LOW FAT / LOW CHOLESTEROL

PREP: 20 min **BAKE:** 40 min **COOL:** 10 min

12 SERVINGS

Have your cake and eat it, too! This moist chocolate cake packs a powerful chocolate punch without a lot of fat. If you like a mild, mellow flavor, use Dutch process baking cocoa, which is less acidic than cocoa in its natural form.

1 cup evaporated fat-free milk

2/3 cup baking cocoa

1 cup unsweetened applesauce

1 tablespoon vanilla

2 cups all-purpose flour

1 1/4 cups granulated sugar

1/2 teaspoon baking powder

1/2 teaspoon baking soda

1/2 teaspoon salt

4 egg whites

1/4 cup granulated sugar

Cherry Topping (below)

Powdered sugar, if desired

Vanilla fat-free frozen yogurt, if desired

Heat oven to 350°. Spray 12-cup bundt cake pan with cooking spray. Heat milk in 1 1/2-quart saucepan over medium-low heat until it just begins to simmer; remove from heat. Stir in cocoa. Let stand 2 to 3 minutes. Stir in applesauce and vanilla.

Mix flour, 1 1/4 cups granulated sugar, the baking powder, baking soda and salt in large bowl. Stir in milk mixture just until blended.

Beat egg whites in medium bowl with electric mixer on medium speed until stiff. Gradually beat in 1/4 cup granulated sugar. Carefully fold egg whites into chocolate batter. Pour into pan.

Bake 35 to 40 minutes or until cake springs back when touched lightly in center. Cool 10 minutes. While cake is cooling, make Cherry Topping. Remove cake from pan. Sprinkle with powdered sugar. Serve with topping and frozen yogurt.

Cherry Topping

1 1/2 cups cherry pie filling (from 21-ounce can)

1/8 teaspoon almond extract

Mix ingredients.

NUTRITION INFORMATION
1 Serving

Calories 255 (Calories from Fat 10)
Fat 1g (Saturated 0g)
Cholesterol 0mg
Sodium 85mg
Carbohydrate 59g (Dietary Fiber 3g)
Protein 6g

% DAILY VALUE: Vitamin A 2%; Vitamin C 0%; Calcium 10%; Iron 10%

DIET EXCHANGES: 1 Starch, 3 Fruit

streusel pumpkin pie

LOW FAT / LOW CHOLESTEROL / LOW CALORIE

PREP: 15 min **BAKE:** 55 min **COOL:** 15 min **CHILL:** 4 hr
8 SERVINGS

Brown Sugar Topping (below)

1 can (15 ounces) pumpkin

1 can (12 ounces) evaporated fat-free milk

1/2 cup fat-free cholesterol-free egg product or 4 egg whites

1/2 cup sugar

1/2 cup all-purpose flour

1 1/2 teaspoons pumpkin pie spice

3/4 teaspoon baking powder

1/8 teaspoon salt

2 teaspoons grated orange peel

Heat oven to 350°. Spray pie plate, 10 × 1 1/2 inches, with cooking spray. Make Brown Sugar Topping; set aside.

Place remaining ingredients in blender or food processor in order listed. Cover and blend on medium speed until smooth. Pour into pie plate. Sprinkle with topping.

Bake 50 to 55 minutes or until knife inserted in center comes out clean. Cool 15 minutes. Refrigerate about 4 hours or until chilled. Store covered in refrigerator.

Brown Sugar Topping

1/4 cup firmly packed brown sugar

1/4 cup quick-cooking oats

1 tablespoon margarine, softened

Mix all ingredients.

NUTRITION INFORMATION
1 Serving

Calories 185 (Calories from Fat 20)
Fat 2g (Saturated 0g)
Cholesterol 0mg
Sodium 150mg
Carbohydrate 37g (Dietary Fiber 2g)
Protein 7g

% DAILY VALUE: Vitamin A 100%; Vitamin C 2%; Calcium 18%; Iron 10%

DIET EXCHANGES: 1 Starch, 1 Fruit, 1/2 Skim Milk

creamy vanilla-caramel cheesecake

LOW CHOLESTEROL / LOW CALORIE

PREP: 20 min **BAKE:** 1 hr **COOL:** 45 min **CHILL:** 3 hr

16 SERVINGS

To help keep the occasional cheesecake drip from leaking out of the bottom of the pan, put the pan on a cookie sheet before popping it in the oven. That way, any spills will be easy to clean up.

15 reduced-fat chocolate or vanilla wafer cookies, crushed (1/2 cup)

2 packages (8 ounces each) reduced-fat cream cheese (Neufchâtel), softened

2/3 cup sugar

1/2 cup fat-free cholesterol-free egg product or 3 egg whites

2 teaspoons vanilla

2 cups vanilla low-fat yogurt

2 tablespoons all-purpose flour

1/3 cup fat-free caramel topping

Pecan halves, if desired

Heat oven to 300°. Spray springform pan, 9 × 3 inches, with cooking spray. Sprinkle cookie crumbs on bottom of pan.

Beat cream cheese in medium bowl with electric mixer on medium speed until smooth. Add sugar, egg product and vanilla. Beat on medium speed about 2 minutes or until smooth. Add yogurt and flour. Beat on low speed until smooth.

Carefully spread batter over cookie crumbs in pan. Bake 1 hour. Turn off oven; cool in oven 30 minutes with door closed. Remove from oven; cool 15 minutes. Cover and refrigerate at least 3 hours.

Drizzle caramel topping over cheesecake. Garnish with pecan halves. Store covered in the refrigerator.

NUTRITION INFORMATION
1 Serving

Calories 175 (Calories from Fat 65)
Fat 7g (Saturated 5g)
Cholesterol 25mg
Sodium 180mg
Carbohydrate 23g (Dietary Fiber 0g)
Protein 5g

% DAILY VALUE: Vitamin A 8%; Vitamin C 0%; Calcium 8%; Iron 2%

DIET EXCHANGES: 1 Starch, 1 Fat, 1/2 Skim Milk

Creamy Vanilla-Caramel Cheesecake

apple-cranberry crisp

LOW CHOLESTEROL / LOW CALORIE

PREP: 15 min **BAKE:** 50 min
6 SERVINGS

Reduced-fat sour cream replaces some of the margarine in the "crisp" topping in our version of the ever versatile apple crisp.

5 cups sliced peeled or unpeeled tart cooking apples (5 apples)

1/2 cup fresh or frozen cranberries

1/4 cup packed brown sugar

1/2 cup all-purpose flour

1/2 cup packed brown sugar

1/4 cup quick-cooking or old-fashioned oats

1/2 teaspoon ground cinnamon

2 tablespoons fat-free sour cream

2 tablespoons firm margarine

Heat oven to 350°. Spray rectangular pan, 13 × 9 × 2 inches, with cooking spray. Mix apples, cranberries and 1/4 cup brown sugar. Spread evenly in pan.

Mix flour, 1/2 cup brown sugar, the oats and cinnamon in medium bowl. Cut in sour cream and margarine, using pastry blender or crisscrossing 2 knives, until mixture is crumbly. Sprinkle over fruit.

Bake about 50 minutes or until topping is brown and center is bubbly.

NUTRITION INFORMATION
1 Serving

Calories 240 (Calories from Fat 35)
Fat 4g (Saturated 1g)
Cholesterol 0mg
Sodium 65mg
Carbohydrate 52g (Dietary Fiber 3g)
Protein 2g

% DAILY VALUE: Vitamin A 6%; Vitamin C 4%; Calcium 4%; Iron 6%

DIET EXCHANGES: 1 Starch, 1 Fruit, 1 Fat

mango brûlée

LOW FAT / LOW CHOLESTEROL / LOW CALORIE

PREP: 15 min **BROIL:** 3 min
4 SERVINGS

Mangoes can be unmanageable to prepare, but they don't need to be. Start by using a sharp knife to cut the fruit vertically in half along each side of the seed. Twist the two halves apart, and cut away any remaining flesh. Then score the mango flesh in each half in crisscross pattern, being careful not to cut through the skin. Flip each half inside out, and remove the square pieces from the skin.

1 medium mango, peeled and diced (1 cup)

1/3 cup sugar

2 tablespoons cornstarch

1/4 teaspoon salt

2 cups fat-free half-and-half or fat-free (skim) milk

1/2 teaspoon vanilla

4 teaspoons firmly packed brown sugar

Place mango pieces evenly in bottom of four 10-ounce custard cups or ramekins. Mix sugar, cornstarch and salt in 2-quart saucepan. Stir in half-and-half. Heat to boiling over medium heat, stirring frequently. Stir in vanilla. Spoon over mangoes.

Set oven control to broil. Sprinkle 1 teaspoon brown sugar over mixture in each custard cup. Broil with tops 4 to 6 inches from heat 2 to 3 minutes or just until brown sugar is melted. Serve immediately. Store covered in refrigerator.

NUTRITION INFORMATION
1 Serving

Calories 220 (Calories from Fat 20)
Fat 2g (Saturated 0g)
Cholesterol 0mg
Sodium 25mg
Carbohydrate 50g (Dietary Fiber 1g)
Protein 2g

% DAILY VALUE: Vitamin A 20%; Vitamin C 12%; Calcium 0%; Iron 0%

DIET EXCHANGES: 2 Fruit, 1 Skim Milk

banana split bread pudding

LOW FAT / LOW CHOLESTEROL / LOW CALORIE

PREP: 15 min **BAKE:** 45 min
8 SERVINGS

Who says bread pudding is just for dessert? For a sweet breakfast treat, forgo the chocolate chips and serve with warmed maple-flavored syrup and a sprinkle of cinnamon instead of the strawberry topping.

1 cup mashed very ripe bananas (2 medium)

1/2 cup firmly packed brown sugar

1 1/3 cups fat-free (skim) milk

2/3 cup fat-free cholesterol-free egg product

1 teaspoon vanilla

5 cups 1-inch cubes French bread

1/4 cup plus 2 tablespoons miniature semi-sweet chocolate chips

1/2 cup strawberry topping, if desired

Frozen fat-free whipped topping (thawed), if desired

Heat oven to 350°. Spray quiche dish, 9 × 1 1/2 inches, or pie plate, 9 × 1 1/4 inches, with cooking spray. Beat bananas, brown sugar, milk, egg product and vanilla in large bowl with wire whisk until smooth. Fold in bread and 1/4 cup chocolate chips. Spread in quiche dish. Sprinkle with 2 tablespoons chocolate chips.

Bake 40 to 45 minutes or until golden brown and set. Cut into wedges. Spoon strawberry topping over each serving. Garnish with whipped topping.

NUTRITION INFORMATION
1 Serving

Calories 195 (Calories from Fat 25)
Fat 3g (Saturated 2g)
Cholesterol 0mg
Sodium 180mg
Carbohydrate 38g (Dietary Fiber 2g)
Protein 6g

% DAILY VALUE: Vitamin A 4%; Vitamin C 2%; Calcium 8%; Iron 8%

DIET EXCHANGES: 2 Starch, 1/2 Fruit

Banana Split Bread Pudding

tropical fruit meringues

LOW FAT / LOW CHOLESTEROL / LOW CALORIE

PREP: 20 min **BAKE:** 1 1/2 hr **COOL:** 3 hr
8 SERVINGS

3 egg whites

1/4 teaspoon cream of tartar

1/2 cup sugar

1 package (8 ounces) fat-free cream cheese

1/4 cup sugar

1 container (8 ounces) vanilla fat-free yogurt

1/2 cup pineapple preserves

1 cup frozen (thawed) fat-free whipped topping

1 cup fresh or canned (drained) pineapple chunks

1 cup sliced strawberries

1 kiwifruit, peeled and cut up

Heat oven to 275°. Line cookie sheet with cooking parchment paper or heavy brown paper.

Beat egg whites and cream of tartar in small bowl with electric mixer on high speed until foamy. Beat in 1/2 cup sugar, 1 tablespoon at a time; continue beating until stiff peaks form and mixture is glossy. Do not underbeat. Shape meringue on cookie sheet into 9-inch circle with back of spoon, building up side.

Bake 1 1/2 hours. Turn off oven; leave meringue in oven with door closed 1 hour. Remove from oven. Finish cooling at room temperature, about 2 hours.

While meringue is cooling, beat cream cheese and 1/4 cup sugar in medium bowl on medium speed until smooth. Beat in yogurt and preserves until well blended. Fold in whipped topping. Cover and refrigerate until serving.

Carefully remove meringue from parchment paper. Top meringue with yogurt mixture. Arrange pineapple chunks, strawberries and kiwifruit on yogurt mixture. Serve immediately.

NUTRITION INFORMATION
1 Serving

Calories 190 (Calories from Fat 10)
Fat 1g (Saturated 0g)
Cholesterol 0mg
Sodium 180mg
Carbohydrate 40g (Dietary Fiber 1g)
Protein 7g

% DAILY VALUE: Vitamin A 18%; Vitamin C 44%; Calcium 12%; Iron 2%

DIET EXCHANGES: 2 Starch, 1/2 Fruit

LOW-FAT COOKING 101: MAKING MERINGUE SHELLS

Meringues are a melt-in-your mouth way to enjoy dessert, without the guilt. These fat-free shells are tailor-made to hold light desserts such as fruit, frozen yogurt or your favorite creamy low-fat filling. Here's how to master the art of making meringues:

1. Beat It!
Beat the egg whites until they form soft peaks when the beaters are lifted. Gradually add sugar, 1 tablespoon at a time, beating constantly until sugar is completely dissolved.

2. Lift and "Peak"!
Continue beating the egg whites until they are stiff and glossy. The egg whites should form stiff peaks when the beaters are lifted.

3. Shape It!
Spoon the meringue onto a cookie sheet lined with cooking parchment paper. Shape into desired shape with the back of a spoon, building up sides.

cappuccino cream parfaits

LOW FAT / LOW CHOLESTEROL / LOW CALORIE

PREP: 10 min **CHILL:** 3 hr
4 SERVINGS

One bite of this creamy dessert is a coffee lover's delight! If chocolate is your passion, use chocolate pudding mix in place of the vanilla, leave out the coffee and milk and use 1 cup chocolate fat-free (skim) milk instead.

1 package (4-serving size) vanilla fat-free sugar-free instant pudding and pie filling mix

3/4 cup fat-free (skim) milk

1/4 cup cold strong coffee

2 cups frozen (thawed) fat-free whipped topping

8 reduced-fat creme-filled chocolate sandwich cookies, crushed (3/4 cup)

Beat pudding mix (dry), milk and coffee in medium bowl with wire whisk about 1 minute or until smooth. Fold in whipped topping.

Spoon half of the pudding mixture into each of 4 glasses. Sprinkle evenly with cookie crumbs. Top with remaining pudding mixture. Cover and refrigerate about 3 hours or until set. Garnish with additional whipped topping and cookie crumbs if desired.

NUTRITION INFORMATION
1 Serving

Calories 240 (Calories from Fat 20)
Fat 2g (Saturated 0g)
Cholesterol 0mg
Sodium 520mg
Carbohydrate 52g (Dietary Fiber 0g)
Protein 2g

% DAILY VALUE: Vitamin A 0%; Vitamin C 0%; Calcium 4%; Iron 0%

DIET EXCHANGES: 2 Starch, 1 1/2 Fruit

Cappuccino Cream Parfaits

creamy peach freeze

LOW FAT / LOW CHOLESTEROL / LOW CALORIE

PREP: 15 min **CHILL:** 2 hr **FREEZE:** 2 hr
8 SERVINGS

This cooling dessert is a sweet ending to a spicy meal. When fresh are available, use four to five medium peaches, peeled and mashed (2 cups).

1/2 cup fat-free cholesterol-free egg product

2/3 cup sugar

1 1/2 cups fat-free (skim) milk

1/4 teaspoon salt

1 bag (16 ounces) frozen sliced peaches, thawed and mashed

2 teaspoons vanilla

2 containers (8 ounces each) peach or vanilla fat-free yogurt

Refrigerate large metal bowl until chilled. Mix egg product, sugar, milk and salt in 2-quart saucepan. Cook over medium heat, stirring constantly, just until bubbles appear around edge. Pour into chilled bowl. Refrigerate 1 1/2 to 2 hours, stirring occasionally, until room temperature.

Stir peaches, vanilla and yogurt into milk mixture. Cover and freeze about 2 hours or until firm. (Or pour into 1-quart ice-cream freezer; freeze according to manufacturer's directions.)

NUTRITION INFORMATION
1 Serving

Calories 170 (Calories from Fat 0)
Fat 0g (Saturated 0g)
Cholesterol 0mg
Sodium 70mg
Carbohydrate 38g (Dietary Fiber 1g)
Protein 5g

% DAILY VALUE: Vitamin A 10%; Vitamin C 4%; Calcium 14%; Iron 4%

DIET EXCHANGES: 1 1/2 Fruit, 1 Skim Milk

chocolate-frosted brownies

LOW CHOLESTEROL / LOW CALORIE

PREP: 15 min BAKE: 25 min COOL: 1 hr
16 BROWNIES

For extra brownie points, substitute peppermint extract for the vanilla in the Chocolate Frosting and sprinkle crushed hard peppermint candies over the top.

1 cup sugar

1/3 cup margarine, softened

1 teaspoon vanilla

1/2 cup fat-free cholesterol-free egg product or 4 egg whites

2/3 cup all-purpose flour

1/2 cup baking cocoa

1/2 teaspoon baking powder

1/4 teaspoon salt

Chocolate Frosting (right)

Heat oven to 350°. Spray square pan, 8 × 8 × 2 inches, with cooking spray. Mix sugar, margarine, vanilla and egg product in medium bowl. Stir in remaining ingredients except Chocolate Frosting. Spread in pan.

Bake 20 to 25 minutes or until toothpick inserted in center comes out clean. Cool completely, about 1 hour. Frost with Chocolate Frosting. For brownies, cut into 4 rows by 4 rows.

Chocolate Frosting

2/3 cup powdered sugar

2 tablespoons baking cocoa

1/4 teaspoon vanilla

3 to 4 teaspoons hot water

Mix all ingredients until smooth and spreadable.

NUTRITION INFORMATION
1 Brownie

Calories 130 (Calories from Fat 35)
Fat 4g (Saturated 1g)
Cholesterol 0mg
Sodium 75mg
Carbohydrate 23g (Dietary Fiber 1g)
Protein 2g

% DAILY VALUE: Vitamin A 6%; Vitamin C 0%; Calcium 2%; Iron 4%

DIET EXCHANGES: 1 Starch, 1/2 Fruit, 1/2 Fat

glazed lemon-coconut bars

LOW FAT / LOW CHOLESTEROL / LOW CALORIE

PREP: 15 min **BAKE:** 35 min **COOL:** 1 hr
12 BARS

1 cup plus 1 tablespoon Bisquick
Reduced Fat baking mix

2 tablespoons powdered sugar

2 tablespoons firm margarine

3/4 cup granulated sugar

1/4 cup flaked coconut

2 teaspoons grated lemon peel

2 tablespoons lemon juice

1/2 cup fat-free cholesterol-free
egg product

Lemon Glaze (right)

Heat oven to 350°. Mix 1 cup baking mix and the powdered sugar in small bowl. Cut in margarine, using pastry blender or crisscrossing 2 knives, until crumbly. Press in ungreased square pan, 8 × 8 × 2 inches. Bake about 10 minutes or until light brown.

Mix remaining ingredients except Lemon Glaze. Pour over baked layer. Bake about 25 minutes or until set and golden brown. Loosen edges from sides of pan while warm. Spread with Lemon Glaze. Cool completely, about 1 hour. For bars, cut into 3 rows by 4 rows.

Lemon Glaze

1/2 cup powdered sugar

1 tablespoon lemon juice

Mix ingredients until smooth.

NUTRITION INFORMATION
1 Bar

Calories 130 (Calories from Fat 20)
Fat 2g (Saturated 0g)
Cholesterol 0mg
Sodium 160mg
Carbohydrate 26g (Dietary Fiber 0g)
Protein 2g

% DAILY VALUE: Vitamin A 4%; Vitamin C
0%; Calcium 0%; Iron 4%

DIET EXCHANGES: 1 Starch, 1 Fruit

Glazed Lemon-Coconut Bars

white chocolate–studded cocoa oaties

LOW FAT / LOW CHOLESTEROL / LOW CALORIE

PREP: 20 min **BAKE:** 11 min per sheet
ABOUT 5 1/2 DOZEN COOKIES

1 1/2 cups sugar

1/2 cup margarine, softened

1/2 cup plain fat-free yogurt

1/4 cup water

1 teaspoon vanilla

1/4 cup fat-free cholesterol-free egg product or 2 egg whites

3 cups quick-cooking oats

1 1/4 cups all-purpose flour

1/3 cup baking cocoa

1/2 teaspoon baking soda

1/4 teaspoon salt

1/2 cup white baking chips

Heat oven to 350°. Mix sugar, margarine, yogurt, water, vanilla and egg product in large bowl. Stir in remaining ingredients except baking chips. Stir in baking chips.

Drop dough by rounded teaspoonfuls about 2 inches apart onto ungreased cookie sheet. Bake 9 to 11 minutes or until almost no indentation remains when touched. Cool slightly; remove from cookie sheet to wire rack.

NUTRITION INFORMATION
1 Cookie

Calories 55 (Calories from Fat 20)
Fat 2g (Saturated 1g)
Cholesterol 0mg
Sodium 20mg
Carbohydrate 9g (Dietary Fiber 1g)
Protein 1g

% DAILY VALUE: Vitamin A 2%; Vitamin C 0%; Calcium 0%; Iron 2%

DIET EXCHANGES: 1/2 Starch, 1/2 Fat

White Chocolate–Studded Cocoa Oaties

chocolate chip cookies

PREP: 15 min **BAKE:** 10 min per sheet
ABOUT 2 1/2 DOZEN COOKIES

1/2 cup granulated sugar

1/4 cup packed brown sugar

1/4 cup margarine, softened

1 teaspoon vanilla

2 tablespoons fat-free cholesterol-free egg product or 1 egg white

1 cup all-purpose flour

1/2 teaspoon baking soda

1/4 teaspoon salt

1/2 cup miniature semisweet chocolate chips

Heat oven to 375°. Mix sugars, margarine, vanilla and egg product in large bowl. Stir in flour, baking soda and salt. Stir in chocolate chips.

Drop dough by rounded teaspoonfuls about 2 inches apart onto ungreased cookie sheet. Bake 8 to 10 minutes or until golden brown. Cool slightly; remove from cookie sheet to wire rack.

NUTRITION INFORMATION
1 Cookie

Calories 60 (Calories from Fat 20)
Fat 2g (Saturated 1g)
Cholesterol 0mg
Sodium 45mg
Carbohydrate 10g (Dietary Fiber 0g)
Protein 1g

% DAILY VALUE: Vitamin A 2%; Vitamin C 0%; Calcium 0%; Iron 2%

DIET EXCHANGES: 1/2 Starch, 1/2 Fat

BAKING LIGHT

There is good news for home cooks who want to cut the fat. Because baking is really a science, in which exact ingredient combinations and amounts are critical, fighting the fat monster is tricky, but it can be done. Fat contributes moistness and tenderness to baked goods, and when there is not enough, the results can be dry, tough, gummy or rubbery.

- Butter, margarine, oil, shortening and eggs are the primary sources of fat. Replacing butter or margarine is a challenge. Applesauce, yogurt, pureed prunes and mashed bananas as well as baby food all work, but none can be substituted for all the fat in a recipe without sacrificing the taste, texture and appearance.

- Overall, applesauce and yogurt work the best in most recipes. They add the necessary moistness and won't alter the flavor as much as prunes and bananas will.

- The flavor of prune puree is especially good with chocolate, spice and carrot cakes. Prune puree mixtures are now sold in the grocery store in the baking section; the label may state that it's a butter and oil or fat replacer (follow label directions for use). Mashed bananas work well in carrot and banana cakes and muffins.

- For the best texture and flavor, we recommend replacing about half of the fat (butter, margarine, shortening, oil) in a recipe with applesauce, yogurt, pureed prunes, mashed bananas or baby food.

- Replacing whole eggs with fat-free cholesterol-free egg product or egg whites is easy. Use 1/4 cup fat-free cholesterol-free egg product or 2 egg whites for each whole egg called for in a recipe.

- Some recipes lend themselves to "baking light" better than others. You may have to experiment a little to find which of your favorite recipes can be modified. In general, low-fat baked goods will be more cake-like in texture and a little less tender than their high-fat counterparts. They also will dry out more quickly, so bake small batches, freeze the leftovers or serve them warm, straight from the oven.

a week's worth of menus

Planning meals can be difficult and time-consuming particularly if you are trying to watch the amount of fat and cholesterol you are eating. Let us show you just how easy it can be! Start by determining your calorie needs. The average recommended caloric intake for healthy adults is 2,000 calories. Your needs may be higher or lower depending on your height, weight, gender and activity level. If you are trying to lose weight, you will want to decrease your calorie and fat intake and increase your activity level. Based on your calorie budget, here are some fat and dietary cholesterol goals to shoot for:

- Total Fat—30 percent or less of total calories per day

- Saturated Fat—10 percent or less of total calories per day

- Dietary cholesterol—300 milligrams or less per day

The menus in this section will help you choose a variety of foods that meet a reduced-calorie, -fat, -saturated fat and -cholesterol eating plan. These menus vary from 1,460 to 1,810 calories, 25 to 33 grams of total fat, 7 to 11 grams of saturated fat and 45 to 140 milligrams of cholesterol per day. You don't have to follow these menus in any particular order. Feel free to mix and match meals from different days to add variety to your eating plan. Just keep track of your total calories, grams of fat and saturated fat and milligrams of cholesterol to assure you're not eating too much or too little. It's that simple. It's up to you.

MENU 1

BREAKFAST

1 serving Cranberry Pancakes with Maple-Orange Syrup (page 188)

1/2 cup blueberries

1 cup fat-free (skim) milk

Calories 410 / Total Fat 3g / Saturated Fat 1g / Cholesterol 5mg

LUNCH

1 serving Smashed Potato Soup (page 154)

1 rye bagel with 1 tsp margarine

Carrot and celery sticks with 2 Tbsp reduced-fat vegetable dip

1 medium nectarine

Calories 495 / Total Fat 11g / Saturated Fat 4g / Cholesterol 20mg

DINNER

1 serving Chicken & Corn Bread Stuffing Casserole (page 64)

1 serving Harvest Roasted Vegetables (page 170)

1 small dinner roll with 1 tsp margarine

1 serving Streusel Pumpkin Pie (page 197)

1 cup fat-free (skim) milk

Calories 645 / Total Fat 15g / Saturated Fat 3g / Cholesterol 60mg

SNACK

1 banana, sliced

1/2 cup sugar-free, fat-free chocolate pudding, made with fat-free (skim) milk
and topped with 2 Tbsp whipped topping

Calories 240 / Total Fat 4g / Saturated Fat 1g / Cholesterol 0mg

TOTAL

Calories 1,790 / Total Fat 33g / Saturated Fat 9g / Cholesterol 85mg

MENU 2

BREAKFAST

1 serving Fruit-Topped Breakfast Bagels (page 183)

1/2 cup orange juice

Calories 180 / Total Fat 1g / Saturated Fat 0g / Cholesterol 0mg

LUNCH

1 serving Caesar Turkey Subs (page 73)

10 reduced-fat potato chips

1 cup grapes

1 cup fat-free (skim) milk

Calories 590 / Total Fat 14g / Saturated Fat 5g / Cholesterol 40mg

DINNER

1 serving Three-Pepper Beef Tenderloin (page 90)

1 medium baked potato with 1 Tbsp reduced-fat sour cream

Mixed-greens salad with 2 Tbsp reduced-fat dressing

1 serving Chocolate-Cherry Sundae Cake (page 196)

1 cup fat-free (skim) milk

Calories 705 / Total Fat 10g / Saturated Fat 6g / Cholesterol 65mg

SNACK

1 serving Baked Tortilla Chips (page 42)

1/4 cup Fresh Garden Salsa (page 44)

Calories 60 / Total Fat 1g / Saturated Fat 0g / Cholesterol 0mg

TOTAL

Calories 1,535 / Total Fat 26g / Saturated Fat 11g / Cholesterol 105mg

MENU 3

BREAKFAST

1 Apricot-Oat Scone (page 182)

1/2 cup sliced strawberries

1 cup fat-free yogurt, any flavor

Calories 310 / Total Fat 4g / Saturated Fat 1g / Cholesterol 5mg

LUNCH

1 serving Curried Tuna Salad with Toasted Pecans (page 82)

1 small dinner roll with 1 tsp margarine

1/2 cup pineapple chunks

Calories 485 / Total Fat 11g / Saturated Fat 2g / Cholesterol 25mg

DINNER

1 serving Quick Veggie Pizza (page 148)

Tossed salad with 1 medium tomato, sliced and 1 Tbsp reduced-fat dressing

1 Chocolate-Frosted Brownie (page 209)

1 cup fat-free (skim) milk

Calories 620 / Total Fat 12g / Saturated Fat 4g / Cholesterol 15mg

SNACK

1 medium pear

4 graham cracker squares

Calories 200 / Total Fat 2g / Saturated Fat 0g / Cholesterol 0mg

TOTAL

Calories 1,615 / Total Fat 29g / Saturated Fat 7g / Cholesterol 45mg

BREAKFAST

1 serving Home-Style Scrambled Eggs (page 190)

2 slices whole wheat bread, toasted, with 2 tsp jam or jelly

1/2 cup cranberry juice

Calories 360 / Total Fat 6g / Saturated Fat 2g / Cholesterol 0mg

LUNCH

1 serving Greek Salad Toss (page 147)

1 cup baby-cut carrots

1 cup fat-free (skim) milk

Calories 535 / Total Fat 8g / Saturated Fat 4g / Cholesterol 25mg

DINNER

1 serving Baked Oregano Chicken (page 53)

1 cup steamed broccoli with lemon

1/2 cup cooked pasta tossed with 1 Tbsp reduced-fat Italian dressing

1 medium slice French bread with 1 tsp margarine

1 serving Cappuccino Cream Parfaits (page 206)

Calories 475 / Total Fat 11g / Saturated Fat 2g / Cholesterol 85mg

SNACK

1 cup Savory Popcorn Mix (page 45)

1 cup fat-free (skim) milk

Calories 205 / Total Fat 5g / Saturated Fat 1g / Cholesterol 5mg

TOTAL

Calories 1,575 / Total Fat 30g / Saturated Fat 9g / Cholesterol 115mg

BREAKFAST

1 serving Mocha Mudslide Cooler (page 184)

1 English muffin with 2 tsp reduced-fat peanut butter spread

Calories 325 / Total Fat 6g / Saturated Fat 1g / Cholesterol 5mg

LUNCH

1 serving Lazy Joes (page 99)

1 serving Tangy Coleslaw (page 161)

1 apple

1 cup fat-free (skim) milk

Calories 480 / Total Fat 8g / Saturated Fat 3g / Cholesterol 25mg

DINNER

1 serving Salmon Teriyaki (page 81)

1 cup steamed asparagus

1 serving Horseradish Mashed Potatoes (page 173)

1 serving Mango Brûlée (page 201)

Calories 630 / Total Fat 9g / Saturated Fat 2g / Cholesterol 65mg

SNACK

3/4 cup small pretzel twists

1 cup chocolate fat-free (skim) milk

Calories 260 / Total Fat 2g / Saturated Fat 1g / Cholesterol 5mg

TOTAL

Calories 1,695 / Total Fat 25g / Saturated Fat 7g / Cholesterol 100mg

MENU 6

BREAKFAST

1 serving Tropical Smoothie (page 185)

1 Raspberry Crumble Muffin (page 178) with 1 tsp margarine

Calories 295 / Total Fat 8g / Saturated Fat 1g / Cholesterol 5mg

LUNCH

1 Chilied Beef Wrap (page 92)

1 serving Couscous Salad with Artichokes & Peppers (page 160)

1 serving Baked Tortilla Chips (page 42)

1 cup fat-free (skim) milk

Calories 545 / Total Fat 11g / Saturated Fat 4g / Cholesterol 65mg

DINNER

1 serving Vegetarian Shepherd's Pie (page 144)

1 serving Buttermilk Corn Bread (page 176) with 1 tsp margarine

1 cup cooked bell pepper strips

1/2 cup apple juice

Calories 450 / Total Fat 9g / Saturated Fat 2g / Cholesterol 5mg

SNACK

1/2 cup reduced-fat frozen yogurt or ice cream with
1 Tbsp fat-free chocolate fudge topping

Calories 170 / Total Fat 5g / Saturated Fat 3g / Cholesterol 20mg

TOTAL

Calories 1,460 / Total Fat 33g / Saturated Fat 10g / Cholesterol 95mg

MENU 7

BREAKFAST

1 serving Hash Brown Frittata (page 192)

2 slices raisin bread, toasted, with 2 tsp jam or jelly

1/2 cup pineapple juice

Calories 470 / Total Fat 4g / Saturated Fat 1g / Cholesterol 5mg

LUNCH

1 serving Southwest Chicken & Chili Stew (page 58)

1 hard roll with 1 tsp margarine

1 cup baby-cut carrots with 2 Tbsp reduced-fat vegetable dip

1 cup fat-free (skim) milk

Calories 590 / Total Fat 14g / Saturated Fat 4g / Cholesterol 85mg

DINNER

1 serving Pork with Caramelized Onions (page 112)

1 serving Sherried Greens with Fruit & Blue Cheese (page 159)

1/2 cup cooked rice

1 serving Creamy Peach Freeze (page 208)

Calories 470 / Total Fat 8g / Saturated Fat 3g / Cholesterol 50mg

SNACK

1 cup Honey-Spice Pretzels (page 46)

1/2 cup apple cider

Calories 280 / Total Fat 2g / Saturated Fat 1g / Cholesterol 0mg

TOTAL

Calories 1,810 / Total Fat 28g / Saturated Fat 9g / Cholesterol 140mg

CALORIE, FAT AND CHOLESTEROL CONTENT OF SELECTED FOODS

Food Item	Calories	Total Fat	Saturated Fat	Cholesterol
BEVERAGES				
Alcoholic				
beer (8 ounces)	95	0	0	0
liquor (1 ounce)	65	0	0	0
mixed drinks (2.5 ounces)	135	0	0	0
wine (4 ounces)	85	0	0	0
Carbonated (8 ounces)				
cola	100	0	0	0
ginger ale	100	0	0	0
sugar-free	5	0	0	0
tonic water	100	0	0	
Coffee (8 ounces)				
black	5	0	0	0
with cream and sugar	40	2	1	5
cappuccino with 2% milk	93	4	2	14
Lemonade (8 ounces)	100	0	0	0
Milk-type (8 ounces)				
cocoa with 2% milk	150	4	3	15
eggnog				
regular	340	19	11	150
light	190	8	4	190
malted milk shake, chocolate	380	15	9	59
Milk (8 ounces)				
buttermilk	100	2	1	9
evaporated	270	10	6	42
whole	150	8	5	33
low-fat, 2%	120	4	3	18
fat-free (skim)	85	0	0	4
soy milk				
regular	80	5	1	0
fat-free, sweetened	110	0	0	0
Tea (8 ounces)	2	0	0	0

continues

CALORIE, FAT AND CHOLESTEROL
CONTENT OF SELECTED FOODS (continued)

Food Item	Calories	Total Fat	Saturated Fat	Cholesterol
BREADS, CEREAL AND GRAIN PRODUCTS				
Bagel, plain (3-inch)	155	1	0	0
Biscuit (2-inch)	135	7	2	1
Breads (l-ounce slice)				
regular	65	1	0	0
reduced-calorie	40	1	0	0
Cereals				
Cooked (1/2 cup)				
cornmeal	65	0	0	0
cream of wheat	60	0	0	0
grits	75	0	0	0
oatmeal	75	1	0	0
Dry				
Fiber One® (1/2 cup)	60	1	0	0
flake cereal, bran, corn and wheat (1 cup)	100	0	0	0
granola (1/2 cup)	215	8	3	0
puffed cereal, rice and wheat (1 cup)	55	0	0	0
sweetened cereal (1 cup)	120	2	0	0
wheat, shredded (1 biscuit)	80	0	0	0
Corn Bread (2-inch square)	145	6	2	37
Crackers				
graham (2 1/2-inch square)	25	1	0	0
saltine (2-inch square)	15	0	0	0
Croissant (1 plain)	325	19	11	75
Dried beans and lentils (1/2 cup cooked)	120	0	0	0
English muffin (1 plain)	135	1	0	0
Muffin, blueberry (2 1/2-inch)	110	4	1	18

Food Item	Calories	Total Fat	Saturated Fat	Cholesterol
Noodles (1/2 cup cooked)	105	1	0	26
Pancake (4-inch)	75	1	0	5
Pasta (l/2 cup cooked)	100	0	0	0
Rice (l/2 cup cooked)	105	0	0	0
Rice cake (4-inch)	35	0	0	0
Rolls (1 average)				
hamburger or hot dog	125	2	1	0
hard	145	2	0	0
sweet	170	5	1	14
Tortilla				
corn (5-inch)	60	1	0	0
flour (8-inch)				
regular	140	3	0	0
fat-free	110	0	0	0
Waffle (4 1/2-inch × 3 3/4-inch)	90	3	1	10
Wheat germ (3 tablespoons)	80	2	0	0
Zwieback (1 piece)	30	1	0	0
CHEESE				
American (1 ounce)				
regular	115	9	6	30
fat-free	45	0	0	4
Cheddar (1 ounce)				
regular	115	9	6	30
reduced-fat	50	2	1	6
fat-free	50	0	0	0
Cottage (1/4 cup)				
regular	55	2	2	8
reduced-fat	50	1	1	5
fat-free	35	0	0	0
Cream (1 ounce)				
regular	100	10	6	31
reduced-fat (Neufchâtel)	75	7	4	22
fat-free	25	0	0	0

continues

CALORIE, FAT AND CHOLESTEROL
CONTENT OF SELECTED FOODS (continued)

Food Item	Calories	Total Fat	Saturated Fat	Cholesterol
EGGS				
Cooked (1 egg)				
hard or soft	75	5	2	212
fried or scrambled in oil	100	8	2	212
Egg product, fat-free cholesterol-free (1/4 cup)	25	0	0	0
FATS AND OILS				
Butter (1 tablespoon)	100	12	7	31
Cream (1 tablespoon)				
coffee	30	3	2	10
half-and-half	20	2	1	6
regular				
fat-free	5	0	0	0
sour				
regular	30	3	2	9
reduced-fat	20	1	1	5
fat-free	10	0	0	0
whipping (heavy)	45	5	3	17
Lard (1 tablespoon)	115	13	5	12
Margarine (1 tablespoon)				
regular	100	11	2	0
reduced-calorie	40	4	1	0
Nonstick cooking spray	2	0	0	0
Oil, vegetable (1 tablespoon)	120	14	2	0
Salad dressings (1 tablespoon)				
blue cheese				
regular	45	4	1	0
reduced-calorie	35	3	0	0
fat-free	20	0	0	0
French				
regular	60	6	1	1
reduced-calorie	25	1	0	0
fat-free	20	0	0	0

Food Item	Calories	Total Fat	Saturated Fat	Cholesterol
mayonnaise or salad dressing				
regular	100	11	2	8
reduced-calorie	50	5	1	5
fat-free	10	0	0	0
ranch				
regular	70	7	1	3
reduced-fat	35	3	0	0
fat-free	20	0	0	0
Thousand Island				
regular	50	5	1	5
reduced-calorie	25	2	0	0
fat-free	20	0	0	0
Shortening, vegetable (1 tablespoon)	115	13	3	0
Vegetable oil spread (1 tablespoon)				
regular	120	13	2	0
reduced-calorie	95	10	2	0
fat-free	15	0	0	0
Whipped topping, frozen (1 tablespoon)				
regular	10	1	0	0
fat-free	5	0	0	0
FRUITS AND FRUIT JUICES				
Apple (2 3/4-inch)	80	0	0	0
Apple juice (1/2 cup)	60	0	0	0
Applesauce (1/2 cup)				
canned				
sweetened	95	0	0	0
unsweetened	50	0	0	0
Apricots				
canned (1/2 cup)				
sweetened	80	0	0	0
unsweetened	30	0	0	0
fresh (3 medium)	50	0	0	0

continues

CALORIE, FAT AND CHOLESTEROL
CONTENT OF SELECTED FOODS (continued)

Food Item	Calories	Total Fat	Saturated Fat	Cholesterol
FRUITS AND FRUIT JUICES (continued)				
Avocado (1 medium)	280	27	4	0
Banana (7 inches)	110	0	0	0
Blackberries, fresh (1/2 cup)	35	0	0	0
Blueberries, fresh (1/2 cup)	40	0	0	0
Cantaloupe (5-inch, 1/2)	95	1	0	0
Cherries				
canned (1/2 cup)				
sweetened	90	1	0	0
unsweetened	65	1	0	0
fresh (l/2 cup)	50	1	0	0
maraschino (1 large)	5	0	0	0
Coconut, shredded, firmly packed (1/2 cup)	235	17	15	0
Cranberry sauce, sweetened (1/2 cup)	220	0	0	0
Dates (3 medium)	70	0	0	0
Fig, dried (1 large)	50	0	0	0
Fruit cocktail, sweetened (1/2 cup)	55	0	0	0
Grape juice, canned (1/2 cup)	75	0	0	0
Grapes, green seedless (l/2 cup)	55	0	0	0
Grapefruit (1/2 medium)	40	0	0	0
Grapefruit juice, canned (1/2 cup)	50	0	0	0
Honeydew melon (5-inch, 1/4)	85	0	0	0
Lemon juice (1 tablespoon)	3	0	0	0
Nectarine (1 medium)	35	0	0	0
Orange (1 medium)	60	0	0	0
Orange juice, unsweetened (1/2 cup)	50	0	0	0
Peach				
canned (1/2 cup)				
sweetened	70	0	0	0
unsweetened	30	0	0	0
fresh (1 medium)	40	0	0	0

Food Item	Calories	Total Fat	Saturated Fat	Cholesterol
Pear				
canned (1/2 cup)				
sweetened	75	0	0	0
unsweetened	35	0	0	0
fresh (1 medium)	100	1	0	0
Pineapple				
canned, sweetened (1 large slice)	40	0	0	0
juice, unsweetened (1/2 cup)	70	0	0	0
fresh (1/2 cup)	40	0	0	0
Plum, fresh (1 medium)	35	0	0	0
Prunes (4 medium)	80	0	0	0
Prune juice (1/2 cup)	90	0	0	0
Pumpkin, canned (1/2 cup)	40	0	0	0
Raisins (2 tablespoons)	60	0	0	0
Raspberries, fresh (1/2 cup)	30	0	0	0
Rhubarb, stewed, sweetened (1/2 cup)	140	0	0	0
Strawberries (1/2 cup)				
fresh	25	0	0	0
frozen, sweetened	120	0	0	0
Tangerine (1 medium)	40	0	0	0
Watermelon (10-inch ×1-inch slice)	115	1	0	0

MEATS (LEAN, WELL-TRIMMED, 3 OUNCES COOKED)

Food Item	Calories	Total Fat	Saturated Fat	Cholesterol
Beef				
chuck	210	13	5	68
corned	215	16	5	83
ground beef				
regular	260	19	8	76
lean	244	17	7	67
extra-lean or diet-lean	176	8	3	64
liver, fried	137	4	2	331
roast				
rib	210	13	5	68
rump	155	4	1	72

continues

CALORIE, FAT AND CHOLESTEROL
CONTENT OF SELECTED FOODS (continued)

Food Item	Calories	Total Fat	Saturated Fat	Cholesterol
MEATS (LEAN, WELL-TRIMMED, 3 OUNCES COOKED) (continued)				
Beef (continued)				
steak				
flank	175	8	3	65
porterhouse	175	8	3	65
round	155	4	1	72
sirloin	153	4	1	72
T-bone	175	8	3	65
tenderloin	175	8	3	65
veal				
chop, loin	140	5	2	93
cutlet	140	5	2	93
roast	140	5	2	93
Lamb				
chop, loin	175	8	3	78
roast				
leg	175	8	3	78
shoulder	175	8	3	78
Pork				
chop, loin	180	8	3	50
roast, loin	180	9	3	71
tenderloin	140	4	1	67
ham, fully cooked	150	8	3	50
Miscellaneous				
bacon				
regular (2 slices)	75	6	2	11
Canadian-style bacon (1 slice)	40	2	1	12
turkey bacon (2 slices)	60	5	1	15
bologna (4 1/2-inch × 1/8-inch slice)	90	8	3	16
bratwurst (1)	260	24	9	49

Food Item	Calories	Total Fat	Saturated Fat	Cholesterol
Miscellaneous (continued)				
Braunschweiger (2-inch × 1/4-inch slice)	35	3	1	16
hot dog (1)				
regular	140	13	5	25
reduced-fat	90	6	2	23
fat-free	40	0	0	11
pepperoni, 1 slice	25	2	1	4
Polish sausage (1)	210	19	7	40
pork link (3-inch × 1/2-inch)	60	6	2	13
NUTS (1/4 CUP)				
Almonds	210	19	2	0
Brazil	220	25	6	0
Cashews	195	17	3	0
Hazelnuts	210	20	2	0
Macadamia	235	25	4	0
Peanuts	210	18	2	0
Pecans	180	18	1	0
Walnuts	160	15	1	0
POULTRY (3 OUNCES COOKED)				
Chicken				
breast, with skin				
broiled	125	5	1	52
fried	175	8	2	64
drumstick, fried, with skin	200	11	3	70
ground	160	6	2	76
roasted, no skin	160	6	2	76
Goose, roasted, no skin	200	11	4	82
Turkey				
breast slices	145	6	2	59

continues

CALORIE, FAT AND CHOLESTEROL
CONTENT OF SELECTED FOODS (continued)

Food Item	Calories	Total Fat	Saturated Fat	Cholesterol
POULTRY (3 OUNCES COOKED) (continued)				
Turkey (continued)				
ground				
regular	200	12	3	75
breast	160	6	2	75
roasted, no skin	160	6	2	75
tenderloin	120	1	0	73
SAUCES (2 TABLESPOONS)				
Barbecue	25	1	0	0
Cheese	65	5	3	0
Chili	35	0	0	0
Hollandaise	90	9	5	24
Lemon curd	80	3	1	0
Salsa	5	0	0	0
Tartar				
regular	150	16	2	13
fat-free	25	0	0	0
Tomato	10	0	0	0
White	50	3	1	2
SEAFOOD (3 OUNCES)				
Clams, canned	125	2	0	57
Cod, broiled	100	1	0	58
Crabmeat, canned	85	1	0	76
Fish stick, batter-dipped	220	12	2	24
Halibut, broiled	100	1	0	58
Lobster, cooked	85	1	0	61
Oysters, raw	60	2	1	45
Salmon				
fillet, broiled	135	5	2	62
pink, canned	120	5	1	47

Food Item	Calories	Total Fat	Saturated Fat	Cholesterol
Sardines, canned in oil	175	10	1	121
Scallops, steamed	100	1	0	27
Shrimp				
batter-dipped	200	9	1	64
canned	100	2	0	147
Swordfish, broiled	135	5	2	62
Tuna				
canned in oil	170	7	1	15
water-packed	100	1	0	26
SOUPS (MADE WITH WATER, 1 CUP)				
Bean with pork	185	5	2	8
Beef noodle	70	2	1	14
Bouillon	18	1	0	0
Clam chowder, New England	90	2	0	4
Cream of chicken				
regular	130	8	2	8
reduced-fat	90	4	1	6
Cream of mushroom				
regular	110	7	2	4
reduced-fat	76	4	1	4
Oyster stew	85	6	4	25
Split pea	180	3	1	8
Tomato	90	2	0	0
Vegetable beef	70	2	1	6
SWEETS				
Candies				
caramel (1 medium)	30	1	1	1
chocolate				
bar, plain (1 ounce)	145	9	5	6
fudge (1-inch square)	90	2	1	0
kisses (7)	175	10	6	8
gumdrops (1 large or 8 small)	45	0	0	0

continues

CALORIE, FAT AND CHOLESTEROL
CONTENT OF SELECTED FOODS (continued)

Food Item	Calories	Total Fat	Saturated Fat	Cholesterol
SWEETS (continued)				
Candies (continued)				
jelly beans (10)	110	0	0	0
lollypop (2 1/4-inch)	80	0	0	0
marshmallow (1 large)	25	0	0	0
peanut brittle (2 1/2-inch piece)	70	4	1	0
Jams or preserves (1 tablespoon)				
regular	50	0	0	0
reduced-sugar	35	0	0	0
Jellies (1 tablespoon)				
regular	45	0	0	0
reduced-sugar	35	0	0	0
Syrups (1 tablespoon)				
caramel topping, fat-free	50	0	0	0
chocolate-flavored	40	0	0	0
corn	60	0	0	0
honey	65	0	0	0
hot fudge topping, fat-free	50	0	0	0
maple-flavored				
regular	50	0	0	0
reduced-calorie	15	0	0	0
molasses	55	0	0	0
Sugars (1/2 cup)				
brown	415	0	0	0
granulated	385	0	0	0
powdered	235	0	0	0
VEGETABLES				
Artichoke, cooked (1 medium)	60	0	0	0
Artichoke hearts, canned (1/2 cup)	40	0	0	0
Asparagus, cooked (1/2 cup)	25	0	0	0
Bamboo shoots (1/2 cup)	10	0	0	0

Food Item	Calories	Total Fat	Saturated Fat	Cholesterol
Beans (1/2 cup)				
baked, no pork	125	1	0	0
green, cooked	20	0	0	0
kidney, cooked	115	0	0	0
lima, cooked	85	0	0	0
soy, cooked	150	8	1	0
Bell pepper, raw (1 medium)	30	0	0	0
Beets, cooked (1/2 cup)	35	0	0	0
Beet greens, cooked (1/2 cup)	15	0	0	0
Broccoli, cooked (1/2 cup)	20	0	0	0
Brussels sprouts, cooked (1/2 cup)	35	0	0	0
Cabbage, cooked (1/2 cup)	15	0	0	0
Carrots, cooked (1/2 cup)	35	0	0	0
Cauliflower, cooked (1/2 cup)	15	0	0	0
Celery (8-inch × 1/2-inch stalk)	5	0	0	0
Corn				
canned, whole kernel (1/2 cup)	65	0	0	0
cob (5-inch × 1 3/4-inch ear)	95	1	0	0
Cucumber (1/2 cup)	10	0	0	0
Eggplant, raw (1/2 cup)	10	0	0	0
Kale, cooked (1/2 cup)	20	0	0	0
Lettuce, iceberg (1/8 medium head)	10	0	0	0
Mushrooms, canned (1/4 cup)	10	0	0	0
Okra, cooked (3-inch × 5/8 inch, 8 pods)	30	0	0	0
Onions				
cooked (1/2 cup)	45	0	0	0
green (6 small)	10	0	0	0
Parsnips, cooked (1/2 cup)	65	0	0	0
Peas, cooked (1/2 cup)	60	0	0	0
Potato				
baked, with skin (1 medium)	130	0	0	0
French-fried (2-inch × 1/2 inch, 10 pieces)	130	7	2	0

continues

CALORIE, FAT AND CHOLESTEROL
CONTENT OF SELECTED FOODS (continued)

Food Item	Calories	Total Fat	Saturated Fat	Cholesterol
VEGETABLES (Continued)				
Potato (continued)				
sweet, cooked (1/2 cup)	130	0	0	0
Radishes (4 small)	1	0	0	0
Rutabagas, cooked (1/2 cup)	35	0	0	0
Sauerkraut (1/2 cup)	20	0	0	0
Spinach, cooked (1/2 cup)	25	0	0	0
Squash, cooked (l/2 cup)				
summer	20	0	0	0
winter	30	0	0	0
Tomato				
canned (1/2 cup)	25	0	0	0
fresh (1 medium)	40	0	0	0
juice (l/2 cup)	20	0	0	0
Turnips, cooked (1/2 cup)	15	0	0	0
Water chestnuts (4)	15	0	0	0
MISCELLANEOUS				
Bac-Os® bacon-flavor bits (1 tablespoon)	30	1	0	0
Broth, ready-to-serve (1 cup)				
chicken				
regular	40	1	0	0
fat-free, reduced-sodium	40	0	0	0
beef	20	1	0	0
vegetable	10	0	0	0
Cocoa, baking (1 tablespoon)	10	1	0	0
Chocolate, baking (1 ounce)	150	16	9	0
Flavored ice pop	40	0	0	0
Gelatin, unflavored (1 envelope)	25	0	0	0
Gravy (1 tablespoon)				
regular	10	0	0	0
low-fat	5	0	0	0

Food Item	Calories	Total Fat	Saturated Fat	Cholesterol
Herring, pickled (1-inch × 1/2-inch)	40	3	0	2
Ketchup, regular (1 tablespoon)	15	0	0	0
Mustard, yellow (1 teaspoon)	5	0	0	0
Olives				
green (4 medium)	20	2	0	0
ripe (3 small)	10	1	0	0
Peanut butter (1 tablespoon)	95	8	2	0
Peanut butter spread, reduced-fat (1 tablespoon)	95	6	1	0
Pickles				
dill (3 3/4-inch × 1 1/4 inch)	10	0	0	0
relish (1 tablespoon)	20	0	0	0
sweet (2 1/2-inch × 3/4-inch)	30	0	0	0
Pizza, cheese, thin crust (14-inch, 1/8)	235	7	4	21
Popcorn (1 cup)				
popped with added oil	70	5	1	0
hot-air-popped	30	0	0	0
microwave 94% fat-free	30	0	0	0
Potato chips (10)				
regular	75	5	1	0
low-fat	84	4	1	0
fat-free	35	0	0	0
Pretzels (1 ounce)	110	1	0	0
Tofu (3 ounces)				
firm				
regular	130	8	1	0
reduced-fat	30	1	0	0
Vinegar (2 tablespoons)	5	0	0	0
Yogurt, plain (1 cup)				
made from whole milk	155	8	5	31
low-fat	155	3	2	15
fat-free	135	0	0	4

Source: General Mills, Inc.

SUBSTITUTION CHART

Choose These	Instead of These	Savings/Benefit
FAT		
Fat-free mayonnaise, 1 Tbsp	Mayonnaise	10g fat
Fat-free sour cream, 1/2 cup	Sour cream	20g fat
Ground turkey breast, cooked, 3 oz	Hamburger (lean), cooked	10g fat
Reduced-fat cream cheese (Neufchâtel), 1 Tbsp	Cream cheese	2g fat
Fat-free frozen yogurt, 1 cup	Ice cream, 16% fat	24g fat
Pretzels, 1 oz	Potato chips	10g fat
Reduced-fat Cheddar cheese, 1 oz	Cheddar cheese	5g fat
Reduced-fat whipped topping, 2 Tbsp	Whipped cream	10g fat
CHOLESTEROL		
Fat-free cholesterol-free egg product, 1/4 cup	Whole egg, 1	210mg cholesterol
Cholesterol-free noodles, uncooked, 2 oz	Egg noodles	70mg cholesterol
Egg whites, 2	Whole egg, 1	205mg cholesterol
Fat-free cottage cheese, 1/2 cup	Ricotta cheese	60mg cholesterol
Imitation crabmeat sticks, cooked, 3 oz	Crabmeat	60mg cholesterol
Low-fat yogurt, 1/2 cup	Sour cream	70mg cholesterol
Margarine, 1 Tbsp	Butter	30mg cholesterol
Fat-free frozen yogurt, 1 cup	Ice cream, 16% fat	90mg cholesterol
Fat-free (skim) milk, 1 cup	Whole milk	30mg cholesterol
CALORIES		
Frozen fruit-juice bar	Ice-cream bar	150 calories
Graham cracker, 3 squares	Chocolate sandwich cookies, 3	80 calories
Hard candy, 1 oz	Chocolate candy	50 calories
Low-fat yogurt, 1/2 cup	Sour cream	150 calories
Pretzels, 1 oz	Potato chips	60 calories
Salsa, 1/4 cup	Cheese sauce	100 calories
Sparkling water (any flavor) or sugar-free soda pop, 12 oz	Soda pop (any flavor)	150 calories
Nonstick cooking spray, 1 spray	Vegetable oil, 1 Tbsp	120 calories

helpful nutrition & cooking information

NUTRITION GUIDELINES

We provide nutrition information for each recipe that includes calories, fat, cholesterol, sodium, carbohydrate, fiber and protein. Individual food choices can be based on this information.

Recommended intake for a daily diet of 2,000 calories as set by the Food and Drug Administration:

Total Fat	Less than 65g
Saturated Fat	Less than 20g
Cholesterol	Less than 300mg
Sodium	Less than 2,400mg
Total Carbohydrate	300g
Dietary Fiber	25g

CRITERIA USED FOR CALCULATING NUTRITION INFORMATION

- The first ingredient was used wherever a choice is given (such as 1/3 cup sour cream or plain yogurt).

- The first ingredient amount was used wherever a range is given (such as 3 to 3 1/2 pound cut-up broiler-fryer chicken).

- The first serving number was used wherever a range is given (such as 4 to 6 servings).

- "If desired" ingredients (such as sprinkle with brown sugar, if desired) and recipe variations were not included.

- Only the amount of a marinade or frying oil that is estimated to be absorbed by the food during preparation or cooking was calculated.

COOKING TERMS GLOSSARY

Beat   Mix ingredients vigorously with spoon, fork, wire whisk, hand beater or electric mixer until smooth and uniform.

Boil   Heat liquid until bubbles rise continuously and break on the surface and steam is given off. For rolling boil, the bubbles form rapidly.

Chop   Cut into coarse or fine irregular pieces with a knife, food chopper, blender or food processor.

Cube   Cut into squares 1/2 inch or larger.

Dice   Cut into squares smaller than 1/2 inch.

Grate   Cut into tiny particles, using small rough holes of grater (citrus peel or chocolate).

Grease   Rub the inside surface of a pan with shortening, using pastry brush, piece of waxed paper or paper towel, to prevent food from sticking during baking (as for some casseroles).

Julienne Cut into thin, match-like strips, using knife or food processor (vegetables, fruits, meats).

Mix   Combine ingredients in any way that distributes them evenly.

Sauté   Cook foods in hot oil or margarine over medium-high heat with frequent tossing and turning motion.

Shred   Cut into long thin pieces by rubbing food across the holes of a shredder, as for cheese, or by using a knife to slice very thinly, as for cabbage.

Simmer   Cook in liquid just below the boiling point on top of the stove; usually after reducing heat from a boil. Bubbles will rise slowly and break just below the surface.

Stir   Mix ingredients until uniform consistency. Stir once in a while for stirring occasionally, often for stirring frequently and continuously for stirring constantly.

Toss   Tumble ingredients lightly with a lifting motion (such as green salad), usually to coat evenly or mix with another food.

INGREDIENTS USED IN RECIPE TESTING AND NUTRITION CALCULATIONS

- Ingredients used for testing represent those that the majority of consumers use in their homes: large eggs, 2% milk, 80% lean ground beef, canned ready-to-use chicken broth, and vegetable oil spread containing not less than 65 percent fat.

- Fat-free, low-fat or low-sodium products are not used, unless otherwise indicated.

- Solid vegetable shortening (not butter, margarine, nonstick cooking sprays or vegetable oil spread as they can cause sticking problems) is used to grease pans, unless otherwise indicated.

EQUIPMENT USED IN RECIPE TESTING

We use equipment for testing that the majority of consumers use in their homes. If a specific piece of equipment (such as a wire whisk) is necessary for recipe success, it will be listed in the recipe.

- Cookware and bakeware without nonstick coatings were used unless otherwise indicated.

- No dark colored, black or insulated bakeware was used.

- When a baking pan is specified in a recipe, a metal pan was used; a baking dish or pie plate means oven-proof glass was used.

- An electric hand mixer was used for mixing only when mixer speeds are specified in the recipe directions. When a mixer speed is not given, a spoon or fork was used.

Metric Conversion Guide

Volume

U.S. Units	Canadian Metric	Australian Metric
1/4 teaspoon	1 mL	1 ml
1/2 teaspoon	2 mL	2 ml
1 teaspoon	5 mL	5 ml
1 tablespoon	15 mL	20 ml
1/4 cup	50 mL	60 ml
1/3 cup	75 mL	80 ml
1/2 cup	125 mL	125 ml
2/3 cup	150 mL	170 ml
3/4 cup	175 mL	190 ml
1 cup	250 mL	250 ml
1 quart	1 liter	1 liter
1 1/2 quarts	1.5 liters	1.5 liters
2 quarts	2 liters	2 liters
2 1/2 quarts	2.5 liters	2.5 liters
3 quarts	3 liters	3 liters
4 quarts	4 liters	4 liters

Weight

U.S. Units	Canadian Metric	Australian Metric
1 ounce	30 grams	30 grams
2 ounces	55 grams	60 grams
3 ounces	85 grams	90 grams
4 ounces (1/4 pound)	115 grams	125 grams
8 ounces (1/2 pound)	225 grams	225 grams
16 ounces (1 pound)	455 grams	500 grams
1 pound	455 grams	1/2 kilogram

NOTE: *The recipes in this cookbook have not been developed or tested using metric measures. When converting recipes to metric, some variations in quality may be noted.*

Measurements

Inches	Centimeters
1	2.5
2	5.0
3	7.5
4	10.0
5	12.5
6	15.0
7	17.5
8	20.5
9	23.0
10	25.5
11	28.0
12	30.5
13	33.0

Temperatures

Fahrenheit	Celsius
32°	0°
212°	100°
250°	120°
275°	140°
300°	150°
325°	160°
350°	180°
375°	190°
400°	200°
425°	220°
450°	230°
475°	240°
500°	260°

index

h

Ham
- Chowder, Farmhouse, 116
- Countryside Pasta Toss, 118, *119*
- Honey, & Black-Eyed Pea Salad, 117
- Loaded Potatoes, 114, *115*
- Panfried, with Sweet Balsamic-Peach Sauce, *88*, 113

Hash Brown Frittata, 192

HDL (high-density lipoprotein)
- effect of exercise on, 23
- effect of fats on, 10–11
- effect of soy on, 141
- effect of walnuts on, 162
- function of, 10, 117
- measuring levels of, 15–16

Heart disease, 7–8, 15–16, 23

High-density lipoprotein. *See* HDL

Honey-Glazed Carrots, 165

Honey Ham & Black-Eyed Pea Salad, 117

Honey-Mustard Pork Medallions, Rich, 108

Honey-Spice Pretzels, 46

Horseradish Mashed Potatoes, *172, 173*

Horseradish Sauce, 141

i

Indian Lentils & Rice, 136

k

Kabobs, Sweet Apricot BBQ Shrimp, *86*, 87

l

Lamb Chops, Mustard, 121

Lamb with Creamy Mint Sauce, 120

Lazy Joes, 99

LDL (low-density lipoprotein)
- effect of fats on, 10–11, 189
- effect of soy on, 141
- function of, 10, 117
- measuring levels of, 15–16

Lemon
- -Berry Brunch Cake, 180, *181*
- Chicken, Provençal, 52
- -Coconut Bars, Glazed, 210, *211*
- -Dill Shrimp, 85
- Glaze, 180, *181*, 210, *211*

Lentils & Rice, Indian, 136

Loaded Potatoes, 114, *115*

Low-density lipoprotein. *See* LDL

Low fat cooking tips
- creamy low-fat soups, 155
- draining beef fat, 102
- fatless broth, 61
- low-fat baking, 215
- low-fat cooking methods, 13
- meringue shells, 205
- steaming foods, 125
- trimming chicken fat, 63

m

Mac 'n' Cheese, Easy, 126, *127*

Mango Brûlée, 201

Manicotti, Vegetable, 132

Maple-Glazed BBQ Meatballs, 34

Maple-Orange Syrup, *174,* 188

Margarine, fats in, 11, 189

Margarine, substitutes for, 215

Meat. *See* Beef; Ham; Lamb; Pork

Meatballs, Maple-Glazed BBQ, 34

Meats, organ, 16

Mediterranean Couscous, 130, *131*

Menus, daily, 217–24

Meringues, Tropical Fruit, 204

Meringue shells, to make, 205

Metric Conversion Guide, 248

Mexican Black Beans with Cilantro-Chili Sour Cream, 146

Mocha Mudslide Cooler, 184

Monounsaturated fats, 10

Mostaccioli, Roasted Red Pepper, 128

Mozzarella & Mushroom Risotto, 133

Muffins, Raspberry Crumble, 178, *179*

Mushroom(s)
- -Curry Bulgur, 140
- & Mozzarella Risotto, 133
- Portabella Gemelli, 129

Mustard Lamb Chops, 121

Mustard Pork Chops, Cajun, 106, *107*

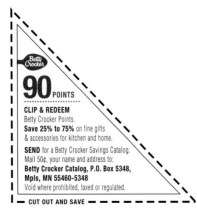